PAPER
CRAFT

PAPER CRAFT

Penguin Random House

Senior Art Editor Gemma Fletcher
Project Editor James Mitchem
Additional design Charlotte Bull, Stefan Georgiou,
Samantha Richiardi, Sadie Thomas
Additional editing Anne Hildyard,
Toby Mann, Kate Meeker
Art Direction for photography Sonia Moore
Photographer Dave King
Consultant Jennifer Wendell Kosek

Managing Editor Penny Smith
Managing Art Editor Marianne Markham
Senior Jacket Creative Nicola Powling
Jacket Design Assistant Amy Keast
Jacket Coordinator Francesca Young
Jacket Quiller Yulia Brodskaya

Senior Producer, Pre-production Tony Phipps
Senior Producer Ché Creasey
Creative Technical Support Sonia Charbonnier
Creative Director Jane Bull
Category Publisher Mary Ling

First published in Great Britain in 2015 by
Dorling Kindersley Limited
80 Strand, London WC2R 0RL

10 9 8 7 6 5 4 3
005–280245–October/2015

A CIP catalogue record for this book is available
from the British Library
ISBN: 978-0-2412-0587-7

Printed and bound in China

All images © Dorling Kindersley Limited
For further information see: www.dkimages.com

A WORLD OF IDEAS:
SEE ALL THERE IS TO KNOW
www.dk.com

Contents

Introduction

Ever since paper was invented in China more than 2,000 years ago it has been used to create beautiful objects – from books, maps, and paintings to flowers and origami. Paper has become one of the most versatile crafting materials known to man, and this book will show you how to use it to create beautiful, personalized craft projects.

For each project we've included a list of all the materials you need, and also supplied templates when called for. We hope you enjoy the book and that it provides you with the skills and inspiration to make beautiful paper objects you can call your own.

Basic equipment

One of the great things about making crafts from paper is you don't need lots of expensive equipment. We'll list everything you'll need for each project individually, but the basics covered on this page are used regularly throughout the book, so they are a good investment.

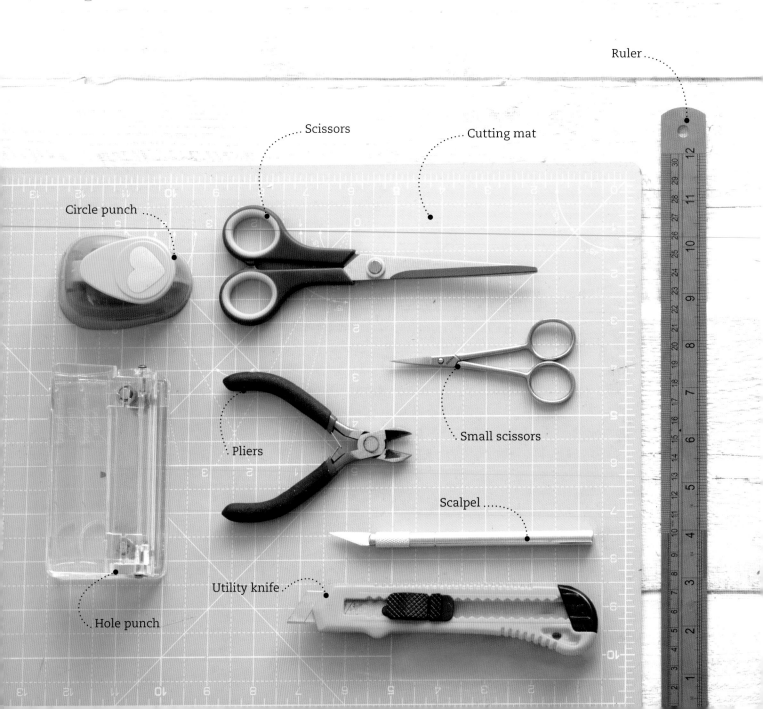

Ruler

Scissors

Cutting mat

Circle punch

Small scissors

Pliers

Scalpel

Hole punch

Utility knife

Assortment
of tapes

Spray mount

Hot glue gun

PVA glue

Hot glue stick

Glue dots

Sticky tack

Glue stick

Scorer

Watercolour
paints

Pens

Coloured
pencils

Pencil

Eraser

Bone folder

Brushes

Types of paper

Flexible and relatively inexpensive, paper is a fantastic and versatile material for craft projects. Here's an overview of the different types that you'll need, and a few details to keep in mind.

Paper types
Unless otherwise stated, the projects can all be made with standard paper or one of those listed on the opposite page.

Weight
The greater a paper's weight, the thicker and stronger it will be. Generally speaking, this will be reflected in the cost.

Style
One of the best qualities of paper is its variety. The number of different patterns and designs available is almost endless.

Colour
Don't feel you have to stick to the colours used in the book. Be sure to experiment and make the projects personal to you.

Tracing paper
Transparent paper used for copying images, tracing paper is used to transfer the templates onto your desired paper or card.

Crepe paper
A thin, pliable paper perfect for making flowers. If you want to make it stronger, stick two sheets together with spray mount.

Quilling paper
Thin strips of paper that are twisted into different shapes. They're available in a great number of styles and colours.

Tissue paper
A very thin, lightweight paper. In addition to being useful for craft projects, it's the perfect material for lining gift boxes.

Origami paper
Usually only one side of origami paper is coloured, but this isn't always the case. The only rules are that it's square and folds well.

Card
Card is a heavier weight than standard paper and is available in various colours and finishes.

Cards and gift wrap

Pop-up bouquet

This cheerful and personal card will bring a smile to anyone's face. It's ideal to send someone special on a birthday or anniversary, as well as being suitable as a get well soon or congratulations card.

Cutting mat

Tracing paper

Coloured card

Scorer

Pencil

Scissors

Double-sided tape

Ruler

You will need

White card, folded in half

Trace all the pieces of the template and position them image side down on the coloured card. Rub over the pattern with a pencil to transfer the image onto the card.

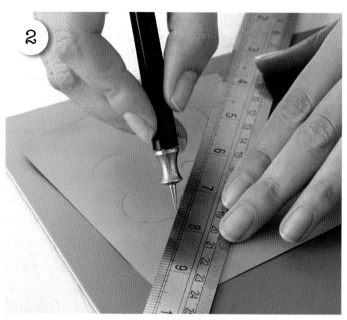

Carefully score along any dotted lines and cut out any solid lines with scissors or a scalpel. Repeat this until you've cut and scored all the pieces of the template.

The four central flowers that need to be assembled are made in pairs. Fold along the score marks and overlap the first and seventh petals to make a cone shape, using tape to secure. Fold in half as shown on the orange flower.

You will need two sets of these flowers.

Stick double-sided tape to two petals and attach a different coloured flower, leaving one petal unattached at either end. You should end up with a shape that is four petals wide and only attached at the middle two petals.

Fold the small pink central flower that is scored in three places and stick one side on the card at the angle pictured above. Peel the backing off the tape on the top edge and fold the card in half so the other half sticks in the right position.

The scored flowers need dots as well.

Using the double-sided tape or a little glue, stick a dot in the middle of the central flower so it sits on either side of the fold. Then stick coloured dots in the middle of all the remaining flowers.

Align with the gutter.

Fold and position one side of the green leaf as shown. It's crucial that the point of the crease is in the gutter and the top edge is 4cm (1½in) from the gutter. Apply tape to the top and close the card so the other side sticks in the correct spot.

Stick the two flowers that have nine petals in position on either side of the central folded flower. Then stick the two large flowers that have six petals to the top edge of the green leaf – one on either side.

9

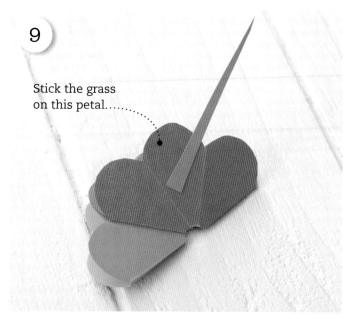

Stick the grass on this petal......

Add a small blade of grass to the back of two of the central flowers that you assembled in steps 3 and 4.

10

Position the central flowers into the crease in the middle as shown. There should only be tape on the bottom petal.

11

This will ensure the flower pops out properly.

Stick the other half of the flower to the other side of the card, but this time add tape to just the top petal. Stick on the remaining central flowers in the same way.

12

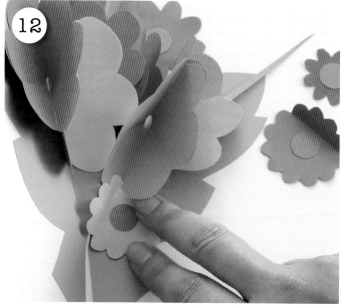

Stick the two medium-sized flowers with score lines on either side of the fold. Then add the little red flower above them, and the little pink one below.

13

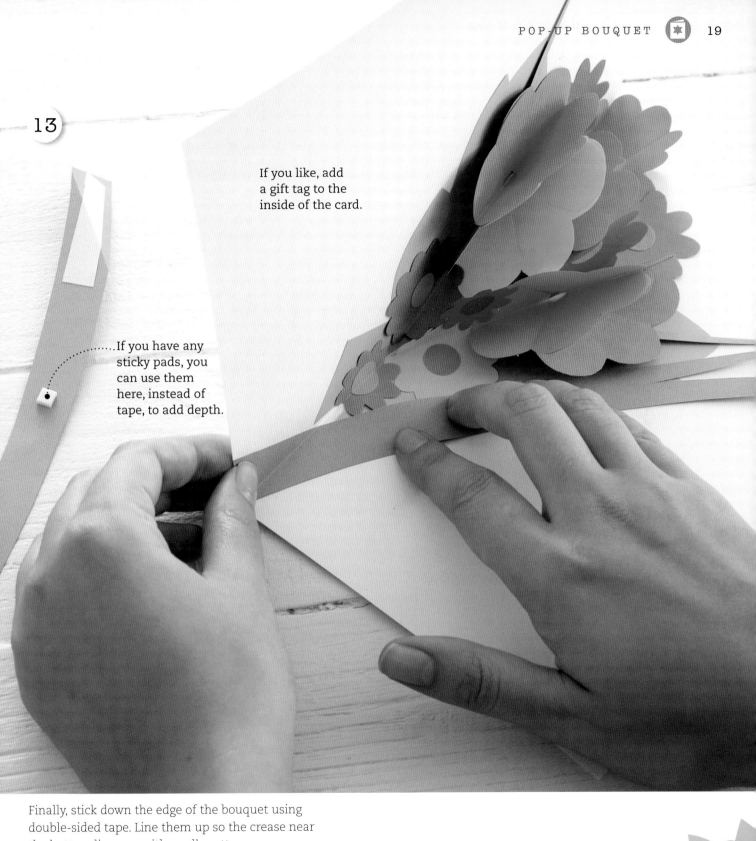

If you like, add
a gift tag to the
inside of the card.

.....If you have any
sticky pads, you
can use them
here, instead of
tape, to add depth.

Finally, stick down the edge of the bouquet using
double-sided tape. Line them up so the crease near
the bottom lines up with card's gutter.

Feather gift tag

Not only are these simple feather tags the perfect way to elevate your gifts, but they also make great little decorations or place cards for a dinner party.

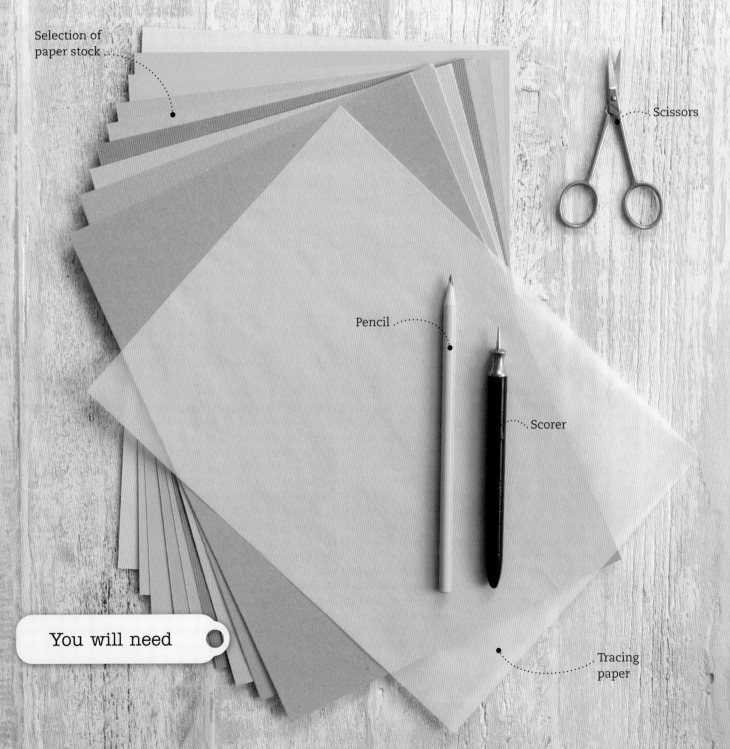

Selection of paper stock

Scissors

Pencil

Scorer

You will need

Tracing paper

1

Trace the templates
and lay them face
down on card.
Rub to transfer.

2

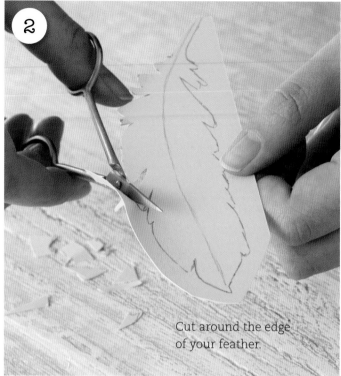

Cut around the edge
of your feather.

3

Score along the
middle of the feather
then pinch to bend
along the scored line.

4

Cut slices toward
the middle to create
a feathery effect.

Tie ribbon around the
bottom and attach to gifts.

DIY envelopes

These little envelopes are the perfect complement to handmade cards, and can be sealed with a sticker, glue, or wax. Best of all, with a little practice they can be made in a flash.

You will need

Squares of paper

Ruler

Pencil

Eraser

1 On the back of the paper, draw along the two diagonals to mark the centre.

2 Fold two opposite corners into the centre, then fold and unfold a third corner.

3 Turn the paper and fold the last corner so it lines up with the pencil and fold line.

4 Unfold the previous fold and align the point with the new fold line as shown.

5 Fold the bottom corners so the edges run along the horizontal fold lines.

6 Pull out the point at the bottom and push the diagonal folds underneath to create a tongue.

7

Fold the tongue over and tuck into the middle.

8 Place your note inside and seal with a sticker, tape, glue, or wax.

Mini gift box

This little box is easy to make and provides a fun, sturdy wrapping solution for all kinds of small gifts. Experiment with different paper colours and weights that will suit your gift.

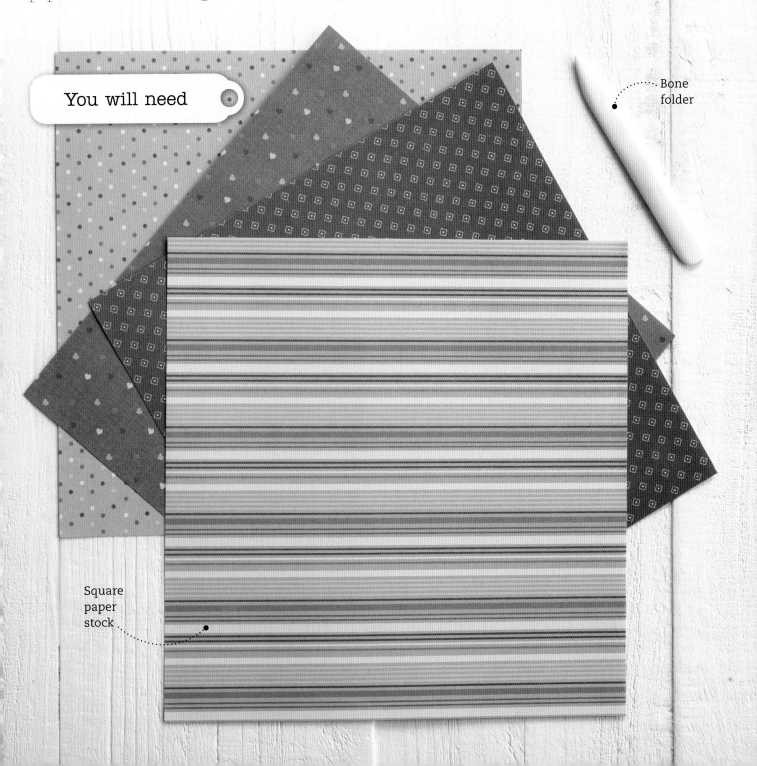

You will need

Bone folder

Square paper stock

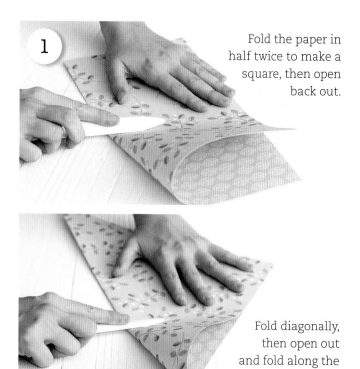

1 Fold the paper in half twice to make a square, then open back out.

Fold diagonally, then open out and fold along the other diagonal.

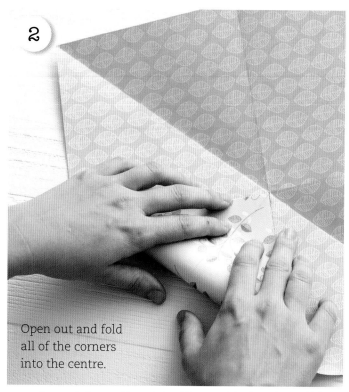

2 Open out and fold all of the corners into the centre.

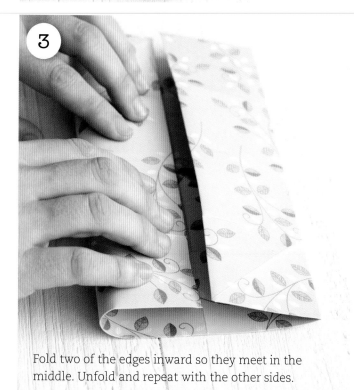

3 Fold two of the edges inward so they meet in the middle. Unfold and repeat with the other sides.

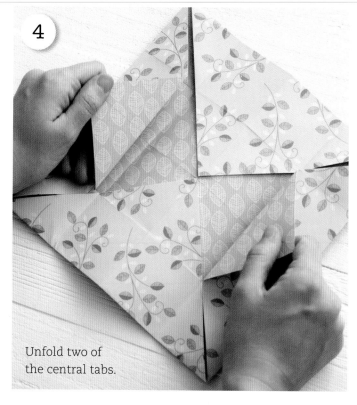

4 Unfold two of the central tabs.

5 Turn the box and lift up the sides.

6 Fold the sides in as shown, then fold the top point into the centre of the box.

7 Turn the box on its side and push into all of the corners to secure.

8 Repeat on the other side, then make the other half of the box.

Use slightly smaller paper for the other half of the box.

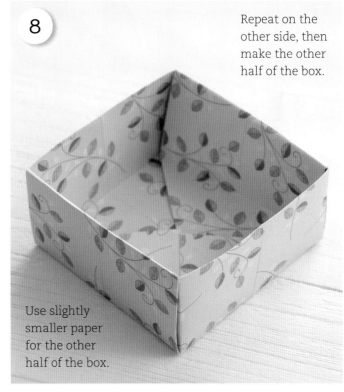

Quilled card

Quilling is easier than it looks, even if it seems intimidating at first.
Once you can make the basic shapes, it's just a matter of gluing them
in place on the card to make interesting patterns.

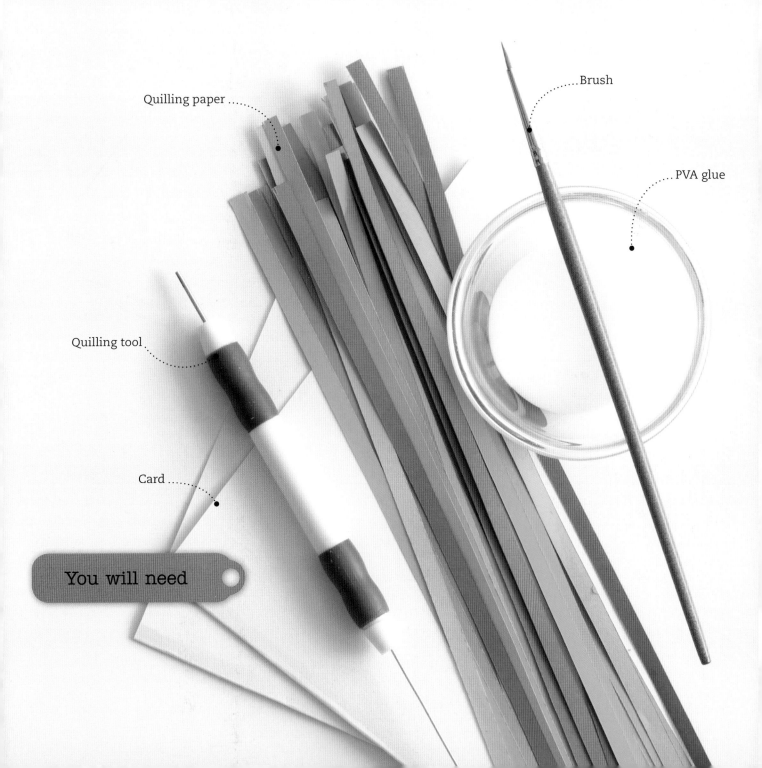

Quilling paper

Brush

PVA glue

Quilling tool

Card

You will need

Tight coil Loose coil Open coil Marquise Teardrop

Coiling

Gluing

> Be quite sparing
> with the glue.

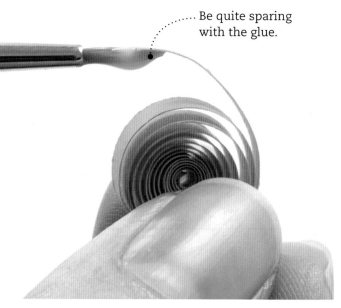

To make a coil, place your paper into the quilling tool so no paper emerges from the other side. Wind the paper around the tool, using your finger to ensure the coil is flat. You can make different shapes by adjusting how tight the coil is.

Use a small brush or toothpick to add glue to keep a coil's shape. If you want to make a loose coil, allow the paper to unravel before applying the glue. For an open coil, let it unravel and don't apply any glue at all.

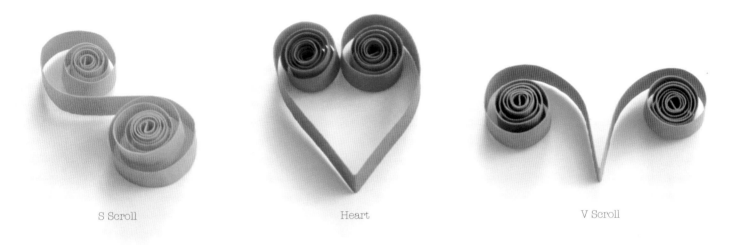

S Scroll   Heart   V Scroll

Shaping

Most quilled shapes are created by making adjustments to the basic coils. For example, to make a marquise you simply create a loose coil and pinch it on either end. To make a teardrop, you do the same but only pinch one end.

Experimenting

Experiment to create the other shapes. For example, a heart is made by folding a strip of paper in half and winding each end toward the centre, and a V scroll is made by doing the same but winding it away from the centre.

Takeaway gift box

If you're planning on giving somebody a small gift, these little boxes are an excellent way to present them. Simply line them with tissue paper and fill with treats. They also work well for favours.

Ribbon

Scalpel

Ruler

Scorer

Scrap surface

Bone folder

Brush

Tracing paper

Hole punch

PVA Glue

Pencil

Cutting mat

Paper

You will need

1 Trace the template and lay it face down on your paper. Rub to transfer.

2 Cut around the edges then carefully score along the lines.

3 Use a bone folder to neatly fold along the scored lines.

4 Make a hole in the four sides using one corner of a hole punch.

5 Fold the box inward, then apply glue to the corner folds as shown.

6 Apply glue to the inside corners.

7 Thread a strand of ribbon through the holes to finish.

Use the alternative templates to create a range
of cases that suit different types of gift.

Attach paper
butterflies to the
cases for gift tags.

Pyramid gift box

An alternative gift box design, this pyramid version is ideal for giving small gifts such as jewellery. They're easy to make and as an added bonus they are entirely reusable.

You will need

Strong paper

String or ribbon

PVA glue and brush

1 Transfer the template to paper and fold along the scored lines. Punch out the holes and glue the edges as shown.

2

Fill the boxes, then thread string through the four holes and tie in a bow to seal.

Customized paper

There's no better way to make wrapping paper, envelopes, and gift boxes unique than by creating customized paper. Here's a quick and simple way to make your own.

You will need

• Pencil
• Scalpel
• Scorer
• Ink pad
• Selection of papers
• Eraser

Draw your design onto an eraser. It can be anything you like, but try not to make it too detailed or it'll be hard to cut.

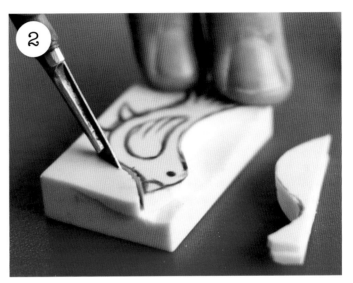

Being very careful, cut around the outside of your design. You want to cut only about halfway through the eraser.

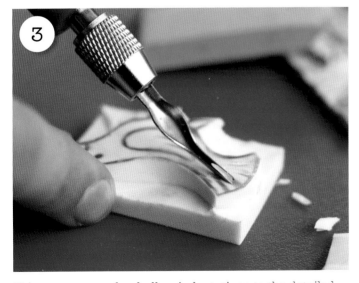

Using a scorer, make shallow indentations to the detailed areas of the design.

Dip your stamp into an ink pad then press onto the papers. Experiment with the position to create different patterns.

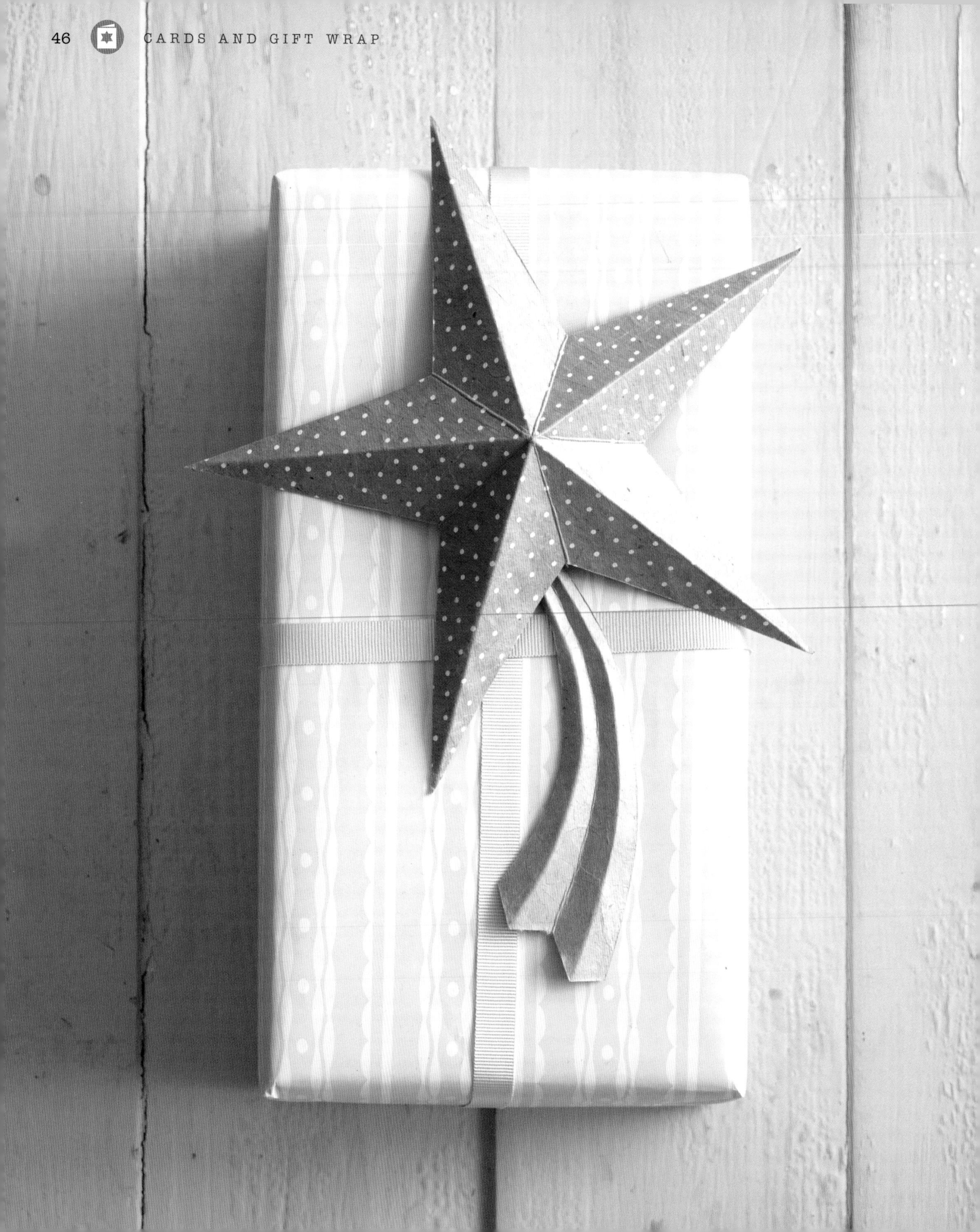

3D star tag

These little star tags are a great way to make your gifts out of this world. They're simple to make, so prepare a big batch and give them to the "stars" in your life when needed.

You will need

- Tracing paper
- Pencil
- Paper or card
- Scalpel
- Ruler
- Scorer

1

Trace the templates and lay them face down on the paper or card. Rub with a pencil to transfer the image.

2

Carefully cut around the outside of the star design. Use a ruler to ensure you have straight edges.

3

Score along the dotted lines, again using a ruler to make sure that your lines are neat.

4

Bend along the fold lines to pop out the star and create a 3D effect.

Gifts to give

Layered papercut

A framed papercut will look great on a wall or side table. Their best feature is their versatility – once you've mastered the basic technique, get creative and come up with your own designs.

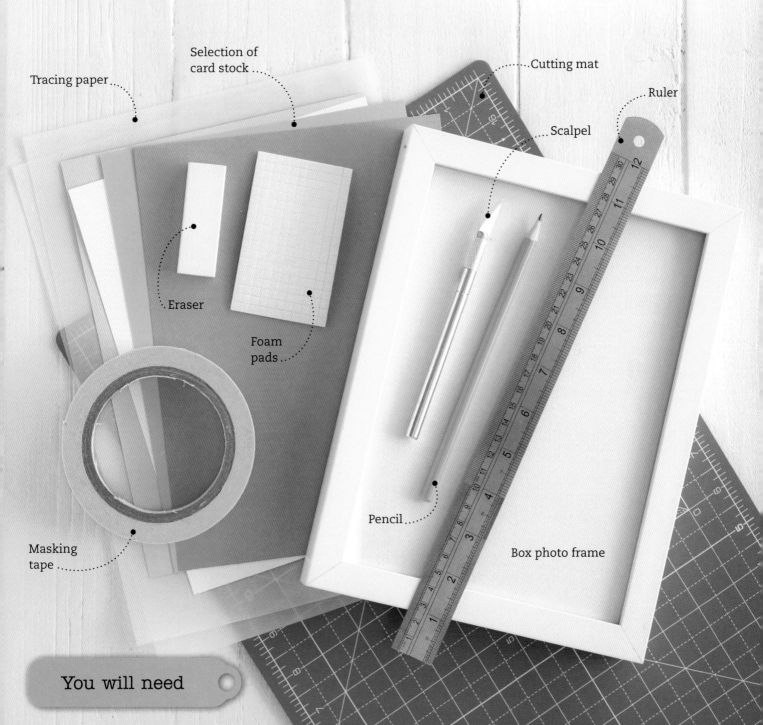

Tracing paper

Selection of card stock

Cutting mat

Ruler

Scalpel

Eraser

Pencil

Foam pads

Box photo frame

Masking tape

You will need

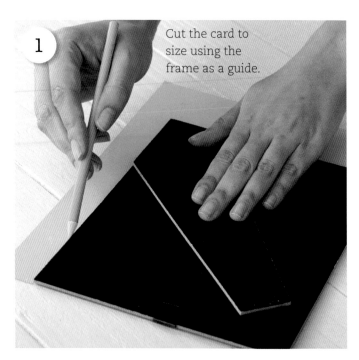

1 Cut the card to size using the frame as a guide.

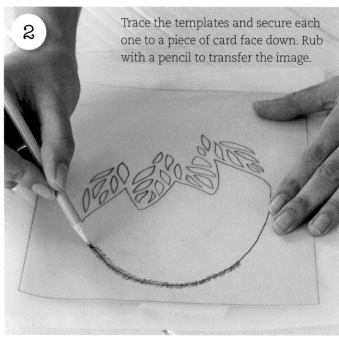

2 Trace the templates and secure each one to a piece of card face down. Rub with a pencil to transfer the image.

3 Using a fresh blade, carefully cut out the small details.

4 When finished, cut around the edge of the pattern.

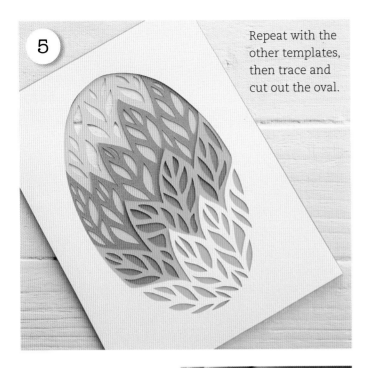

5 Repeat with the other templates, then trace and cut out the oval.

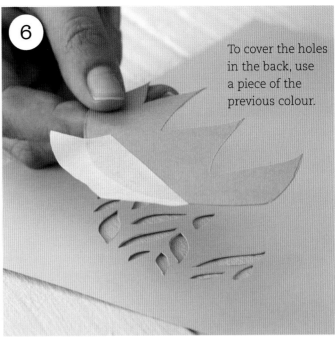

6 To cover the holes in the back, use a piece of the previous colour.

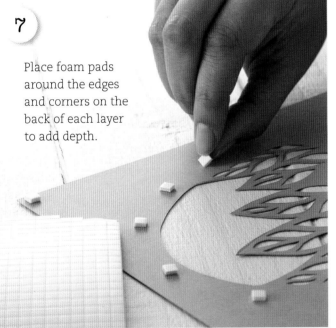

7 Place foam pads around the edges and corners on the back of each layer to add depth.

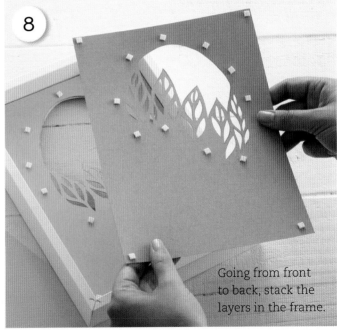

8 Going from front to back, stack the layers in the frame.

To vary the papercut, design your own template using different flower shapes. Alternatively, you can remove the foam pads to create a flat design.

Layered papercuts can be made to suit almost any frame.

Quilled earrings

The art of quilling has been around for centuries, but this modern twist makes for a perfect gift. You can easily customize the shapes to make your own designs.

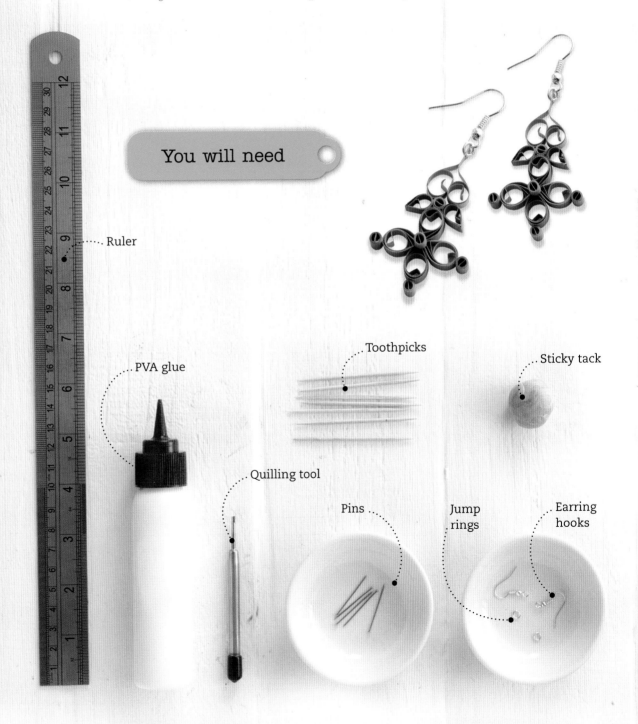

Dark and light strips of quilling paper

You will need

Ruler

PVA glue

Toothpicks

Sticky tack

Quilling tool

Pins

Jump rings

Earring hooks

1

Cut the dark green quilling strips into two 10cm (4in) and four 5cm (2in) strips. Then cut the light green strips into three 10cm (4in) and three 5cm (2in) strips.

2

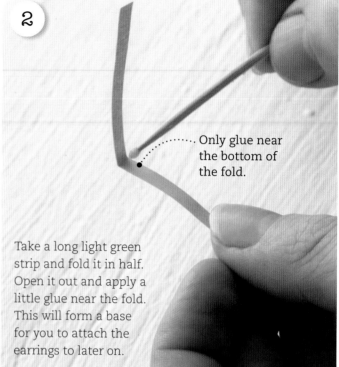

Only glue near the bottom of the fold.

Take a long light green strip and fold it in half. Open it out and apply a little glue near the fold. This will form a base for you to attach the earrings to later on.

3

Insert one end of the strip into the tool and twist it toward the fold, leaving a small gap at the end. Release and repeat with the other side to create a heart.

When finished, glue together

4

Take a short light strip and twist it into a tight coil. Glue the end down and slide it off the tool. Repeat with the remaining short light strips and two dark ones.

5

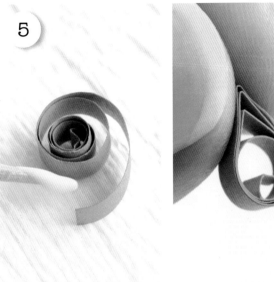

Twirl one of the long dark strips into a coil, then release and glue in place.

Pinch one of the ends to make a teardrop shape. Repeat this with the remaining long and short strips.

6

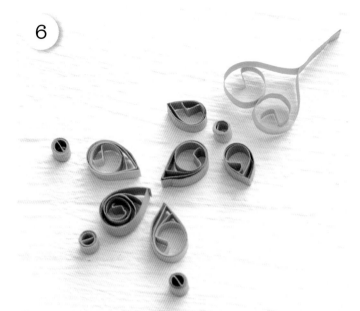

Arrange your pieces on a surface, keeping one small coil in reserve. If you like you can try a different shape, but make sure it's strong enough to hold together.

7

Carefully glue the pieces together using a toothpick (tweezers can also help). Go slowly, allowing each piece to dry before adding the next.

Glue the reserved coil on top

8

Place the base of the heart on the sticky tack, and use a pin to make a hole. Thread a jump ring through the hole and then attach an earring hook. Repeat for the second earring.

Nursery papercut

This charming papercut is deceptively simple to put together, and will make a lovely decoration for a nursery or young child's bedroom. It's easily adaptable, so tailor your papercut's subject and size to whatever you wish.

You will need

Cutting mat

Ruler

Eraser

Frame

Pencil

Scalpel

White card

Acetate

Tracing paper

Coloured card

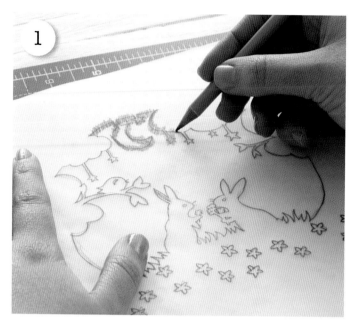

Using a pencil, transfer the template to tracing paper and turn it over. Lay it on top of your card and rub over the tracing with pencil to transfer the image onto the card.

Use small cuts for the curves.

Using a fresh blade, carefully start cutting the smaller, fiddly areas of the picture such as the eyes, arms, and the inside of the ears.

Take your time to ensure the cuts are neat.

Working in a clockwise direction, cut one side of each petal at the bottom towards the centre of each flower. Then cut the other side of each petal working in the other direction.

Cut away from the joins to avoid over cutting.

Turn the image upside down and cut out the grass. When this is complete, carefully cut away the remaining paper between the rabbits.

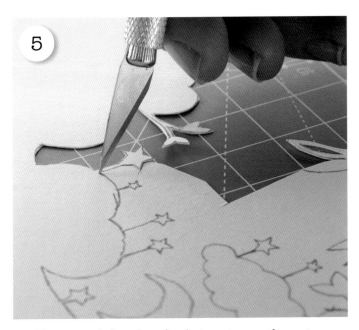

Working around the edges, begin to cut away the rest of the image. Take your time, especially with smaller areas such as the stars and leaves.

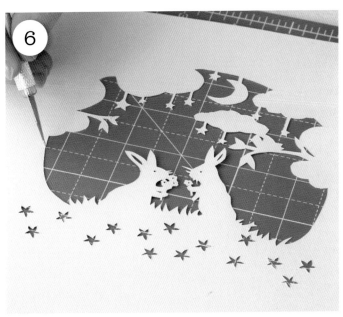

Once you have finished cutting all of the image away, flip the card over and go back over any snagged areas to tidy them up

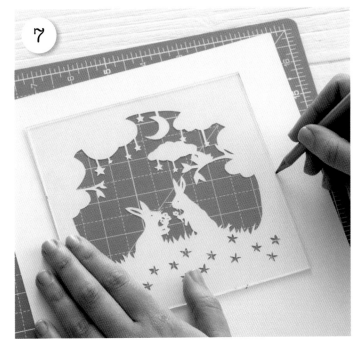

Measure the size of the glass in your frame and cut the image, acetate, and background card to this size. Use the glass to ensure the image is central to the markings.

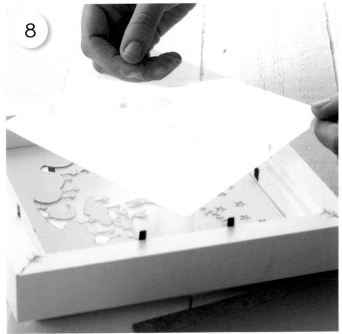

Place the glass and image in the frame, followed by the acetate. Add the frame insert and lay the background card on top before affixing the back of the frame in place.

Papercut locket

With a little creativity, patience, and a very steady hand, you can adapt the same technique used for the nursery papercut to make something small enough to fit in a locket or a keyring.

Make sure the design can fit inside the locket.

Almost any simple shape will work, but as the papercut needs to be small, choose something without too much detail or it will be very hard to cut neatly.

Use a repositionable glue so it doesn't smear the glass.

Papercut lantern

These stylish hand-cut lanterns will produce a lovely gentle glow and will look great on any mantelpiece. They also make perfect table decorations for a dinner party or wedding.

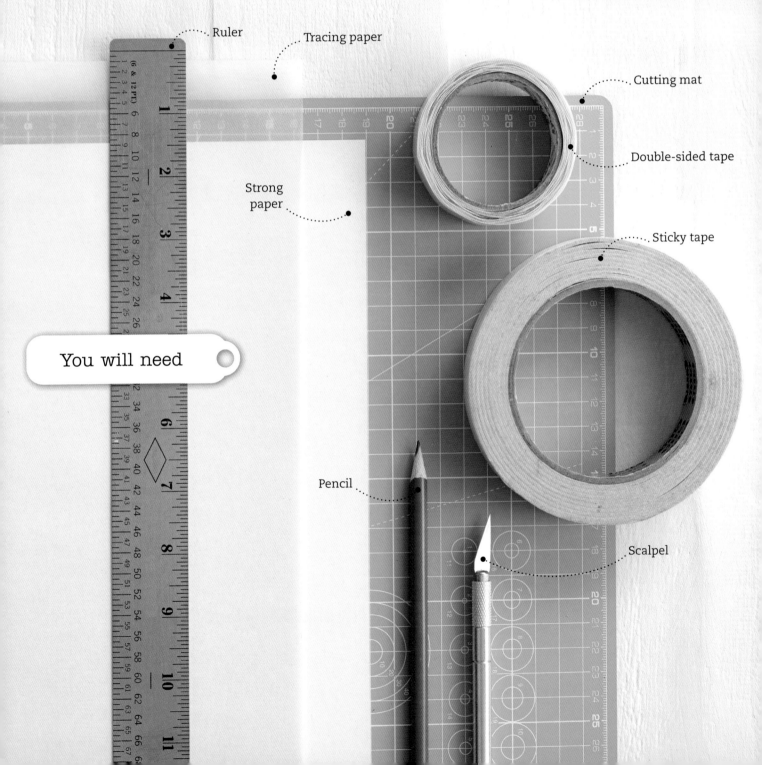

Ruler

Tracing paper

Cutting mat

Double-sided tape

Strong paper

Sticky tape

You will need

Pencil

Scalpel

Prepare your template and begin to cut away the inside of one of the four panels. Make sure you keep the template right-side up during the whole cutting process.

Once you've finished cutting the inside of the first panel, cut out the pattern above it. Repeat this process, going from one side of the template to the other.

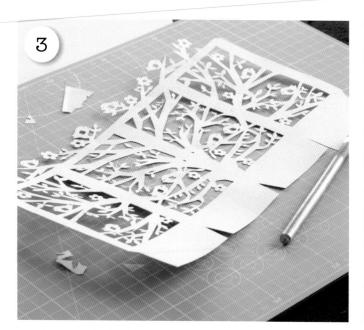

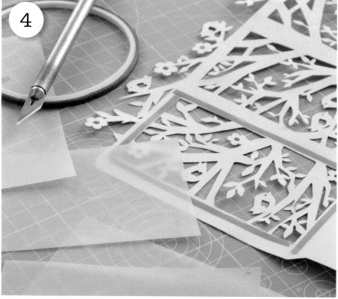

Continue until all of the excess paper has been cut away. You may need to change your blade several times to avoid creating frayed edges.

Apply thin double-sided tape to the edges of the panels. Before peeling off the second side, measure and cut four tracing paper rectangles the same size as the tape's border.

Peel back the other half of the tape and carefully stick the tracing paper on top. Repeat this process until the tracing paper covers all four panels.

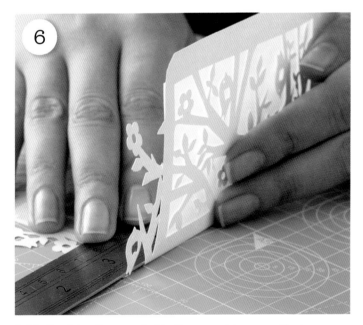

Fold all of the flaps and side lines, making sure that there's a stiff crease on all the edges. This will ensure that the lantern will stand up straight when finished.

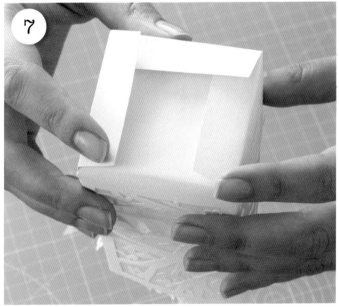

Glue or tape all of the flaps in place, holding them in position for a short while to make sure they stick properly. To finish, add a flameless candle or fairy lights.

You can also create papercut lanterns by wrapping coloured tracing paper around a vase and placing the papercut on top.

Don't feel like you have to only make dark silhouettes. These also work surprisingly well with card that is brightly-coloured.

Silhouette frame

A modern take on the classic family portrait, a silhouette gallery is simple to put together and can make an instant impression. They're also a great way to repurpose old photos.

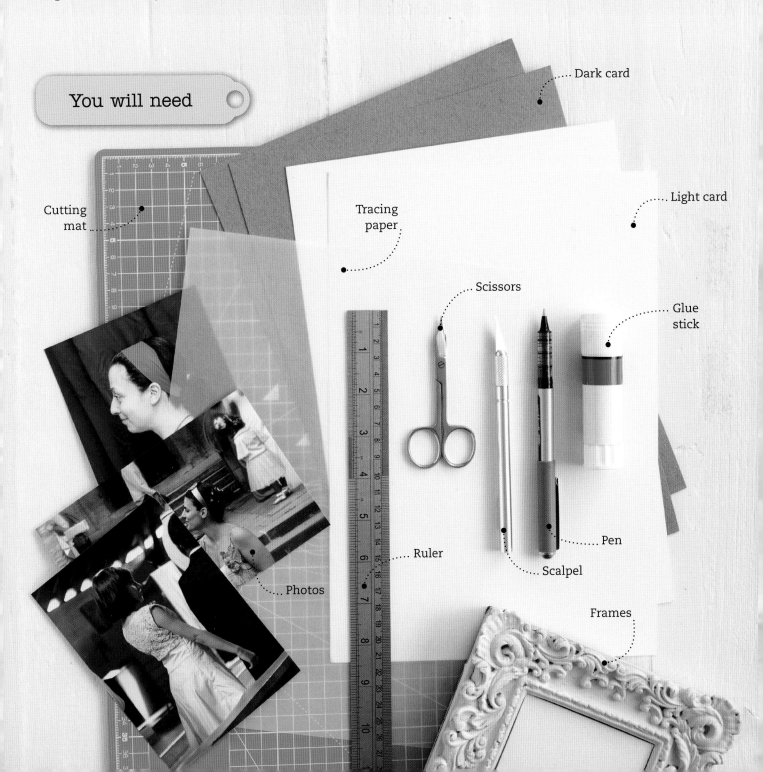

You will need

Dark card

Cutting mat

Tracing paper

Light card

Scissors

Glue stick

Ruler

Pen

Scalpel

Photos

Frames

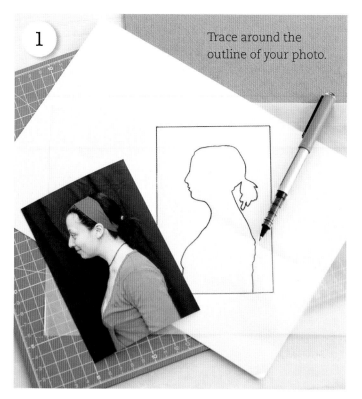

1 Trace around the outline of your photo.

2 Apply glue to the back of the tracing.

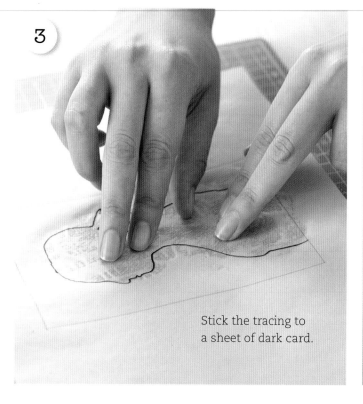

3 Stick the tracing to a sheet of dark card.

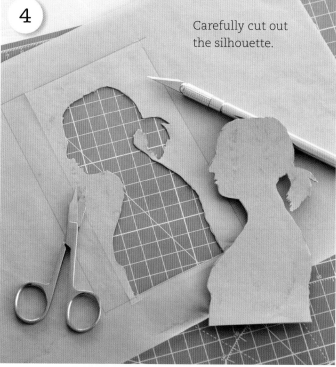

4 Carefully cut out the silhouette.

5

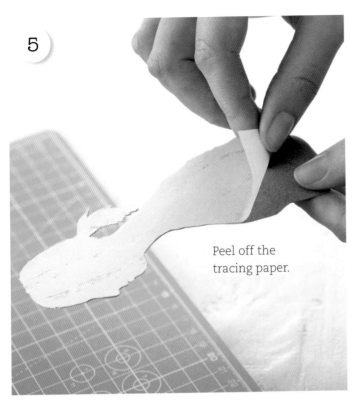

Peel off the tracing paper.

6

Mark the outline of your frame on a sheet of light card and apply glue to your silhouette.

7

Stick your silhouette in the centre of your frame's outline.

8

Carefully cut around the frame's outline and mount it in the frame.

Decorations

Honeycomb pom-pom

These appealing pom-poms can liven up any room, and are perfect for a party, wedding, or just as decorations for a room. They work well in both bright and pastel colours.

You will need

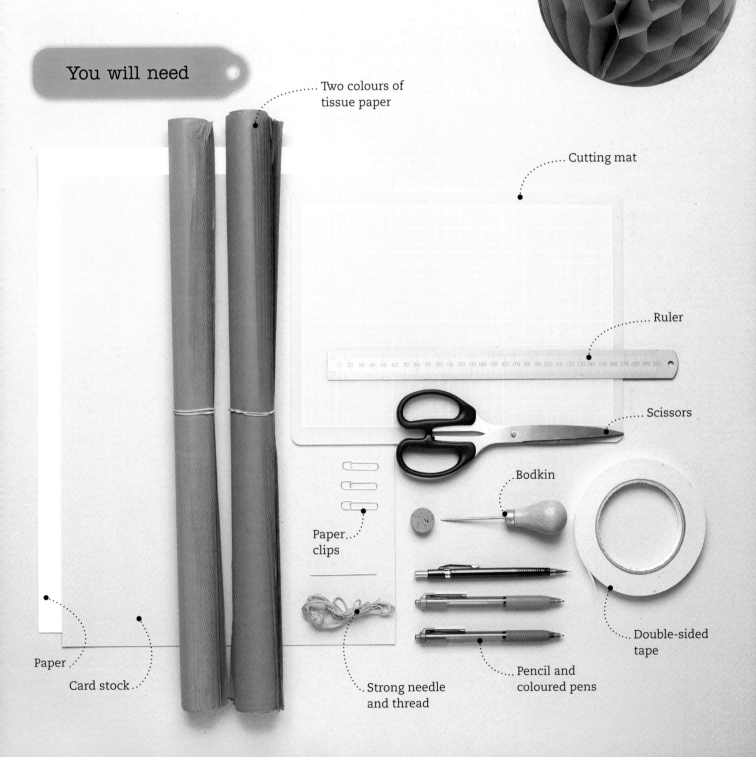

Two colours of tissue paper

Cutting mat

Ruler

Scissors

Bodkin

Paper clips

Double-sided tape

Paper

Card stock

Strong needle and thread

Pencil and coloured pens

1

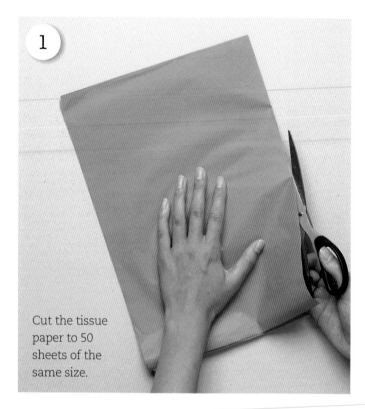

Cut the tissue paper to 50 sheets of the same size.

2

Cut a sheet of card slightly larger than your sheets. Mark the top and bottom edges, leaving a 1cm (½in) border, then divide the space inside into five equally-spaced lines.

3

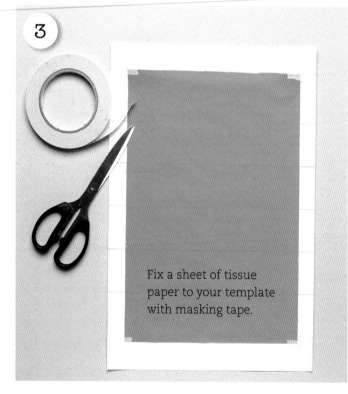

Fix a sheet of tissue paper to your template with masking tape.

4

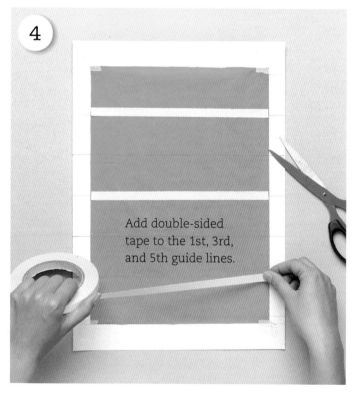

Add double-sided tape to the 1st, 3rd, and 5th guide lines.

5

Stick down five sheets of one colour, then three of another, alternating between the odd and even guide lines every time.

6

Cut a semi circle from card that lines up with your outer borders and draw around it.

7

Carefully cut out all your sheets.

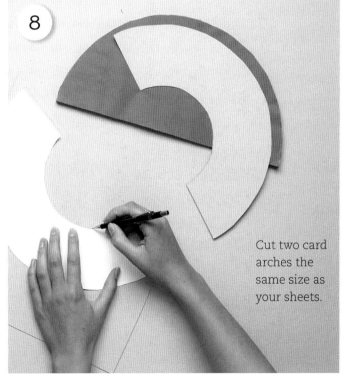

8

Cut two card arches the same size as your sheets.

9

Tape or glue an arch to either side of your sheets.

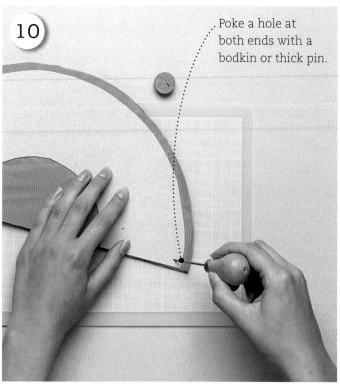

10

Poke a hole at both ends with a bodkin or thick pin.

11

Pull and knot thread through the holes, but leave a little slack so the pom-pom can open.

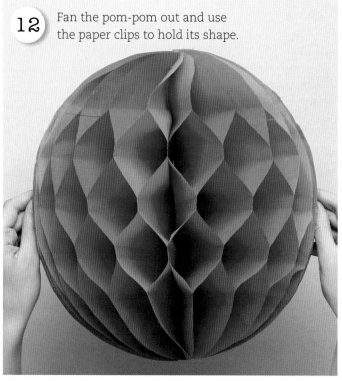

12

Fan the pom-pom out and use the paper clips to hold its shape.

13

Hang the pom-
poms from the
knotted thread.

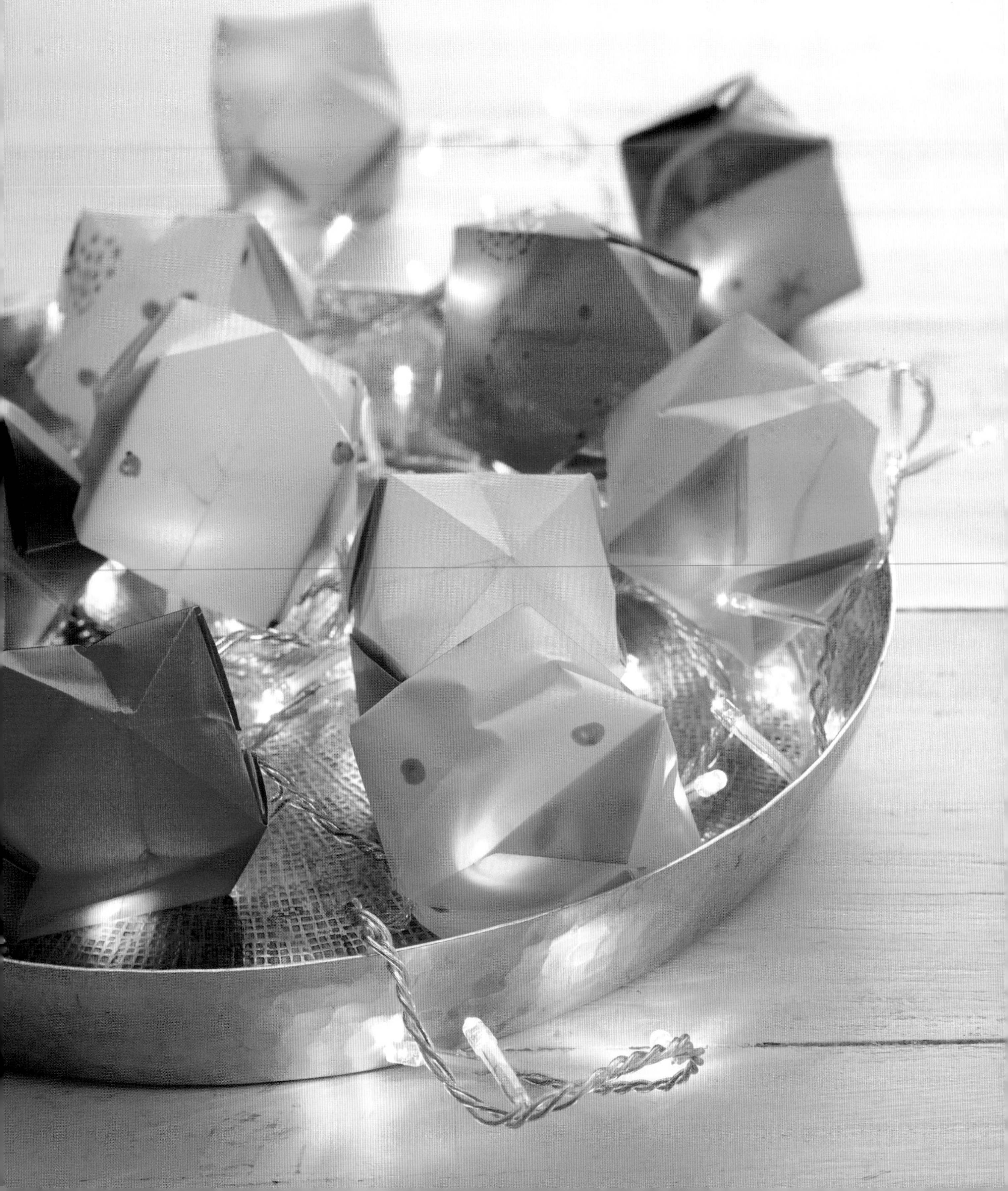

Origami fairy lights

Whether the holiday season is right around the corner or you're just looking to brighten up a room, these fairy lights will do the trick. Depending how strong your LED lights are, you may need to experiment with a variety of paper opacity to get the right look.

You will need

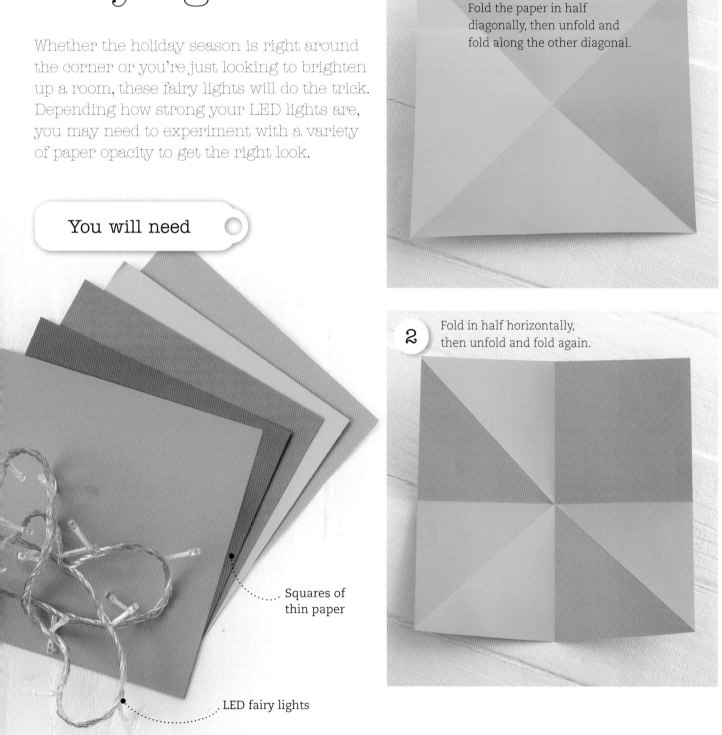

Squares of thin paper

LED fairy lights

1 Fold the paper in half diagonally, then unfold and fold along the other diagonal.

2 Fold in half horizontally, then unfold and fold again.

3 Turn the paper over.

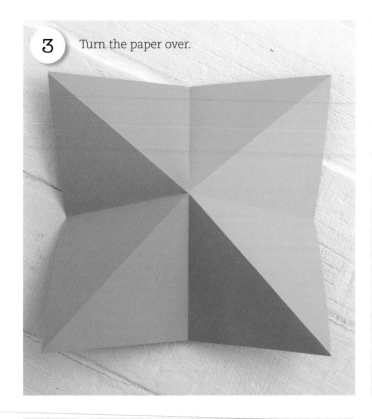

4 Push in the right and left horizontal folds, then flatten to create a layered triangle shape.

5 Fold up the bottom corners as shown, then repeat on the back to form a diamond.

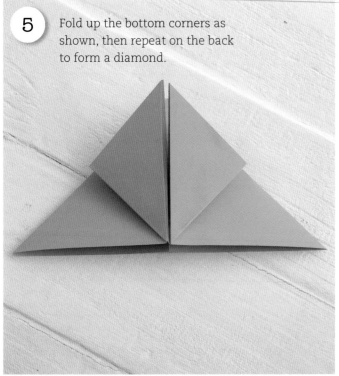

6

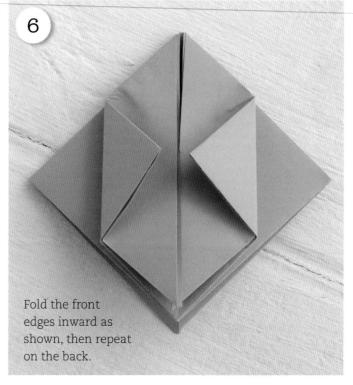

Fold the front edges inward as shown, then repeat on the back.

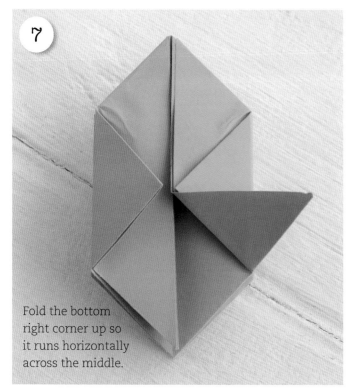

7 Fold the bottom right corner up so it runs horizontally across the middle.

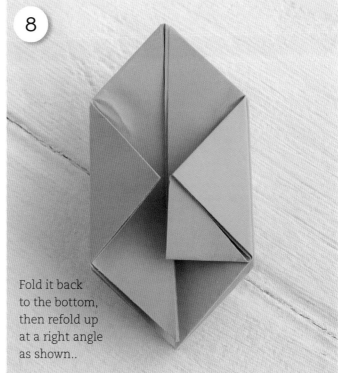

8 Fold it back to the bottom, then refold up at a right angle as shown..

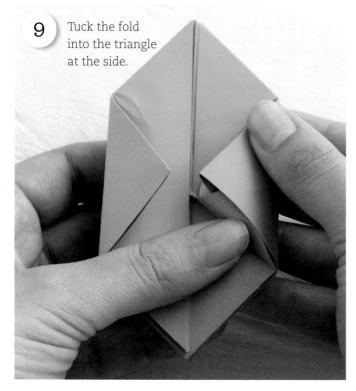

9 Tuck the fold into the triangle at the side.

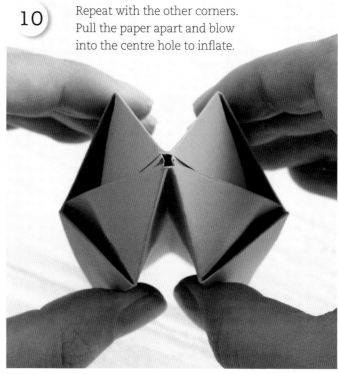

10 Repeat with the other corners. Pull the paper apart and blow into the centre hole to inflate.

Hanging fan

These bright, bold fans can take a while to put together, but the results are stunning. By making several in a variety of colours and sizes you'll be able to create a striking wall display.

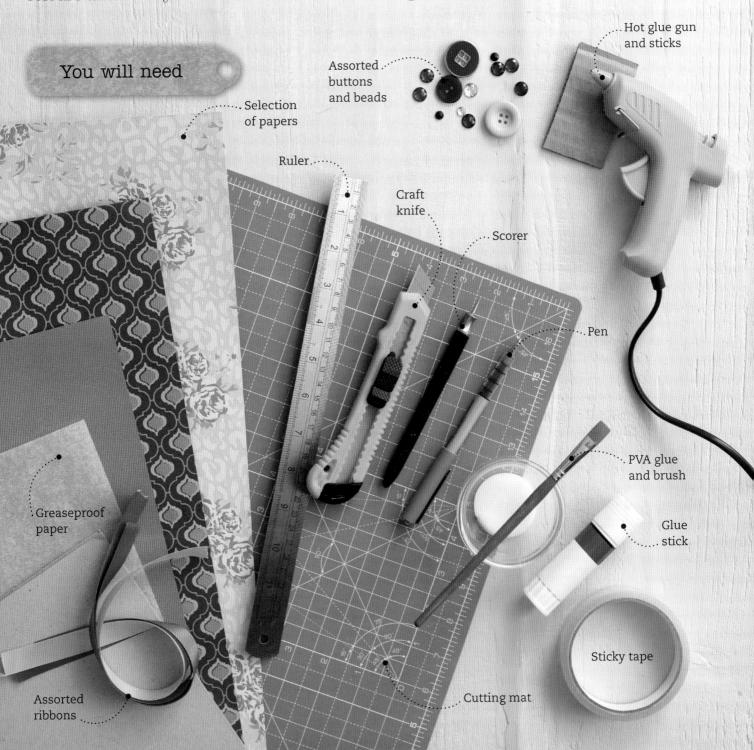

You will need

Selection of papers

Assorted buttons and beads

Hot glue gun and sticks

Ruler

Craft knife

Scorer

Pen

PVA glue and brush

Glue stick

Greaseproof paper

Sticky tape

Assorted ribbons

Cutting mat

Score equally-spaced vertical lines on several sheets of paper. The more sheets you use and the wider the lines, the bigger the fan will be. Use the guides on your cutting mat to make sure the lines are straight.

Apply PVA glue to the bottom segment of one of the sheets of paper. Stick the top segment of another sheet of paper on top so they overlap. Allow to dry and then repeat with the other sheets (minimum of two).

Fold the papers along the scored creases to create an accordion effect.

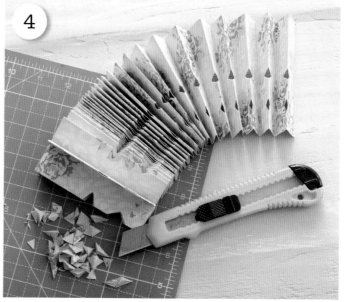

Repeat this process with slimmer sheets of paper of a different colour. When done, lay them flat and cut shapes into the folds to add detail.

5

Repeat again with another thinner paper. However, instead of cutting a design in the folds, slice the ends off diagonally.

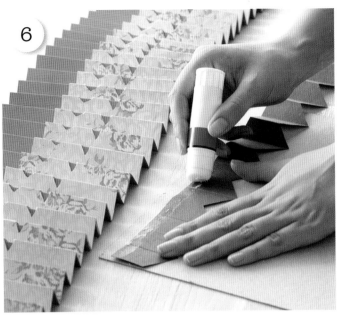

6

Use a glue stick to attach the second paper to the first and allow to dry. Then apply glue to the bottom of the third.

7

Glue the third paper along the bottom edge of the fan. Take your time to ensure the edges align properly.

Make sure to glue firmly.

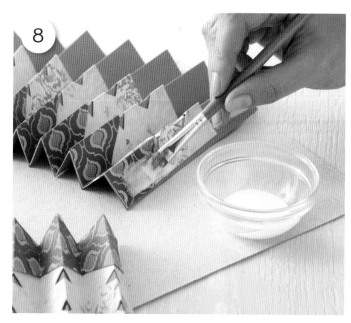

Apply PVA glue to one of the ends, then bring the two sides of the accordion together to form a large circle.

Lay the fan on greaseproof paper and use a hot glue gun to create a pool of glue in the centre.

Using both hands, carefully squeeze the fan inward so the centre moves toward the glue and shrinks. Hold in place until the glue sets then peel away the greaseproof paper.

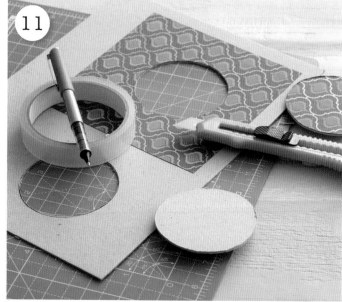

Use the inside ring of a roll of sticky tape to mark two discs from card. One should be plain, and the other one should have coloured paper stuck to it. Neatly cut out the discs.

12

Turn the fan on its back and stick the plain disc to the centre with hot glue. Fold a ribbon in half, place the opposite ends on top, then stick the second disc on top with more hot glue.

13

Lay the folded ribbon between one of the fan's folds, then secure in place with a strip of paper and some PVA glue.

14 Cover the hole on the front of your fan with buttons or beads.

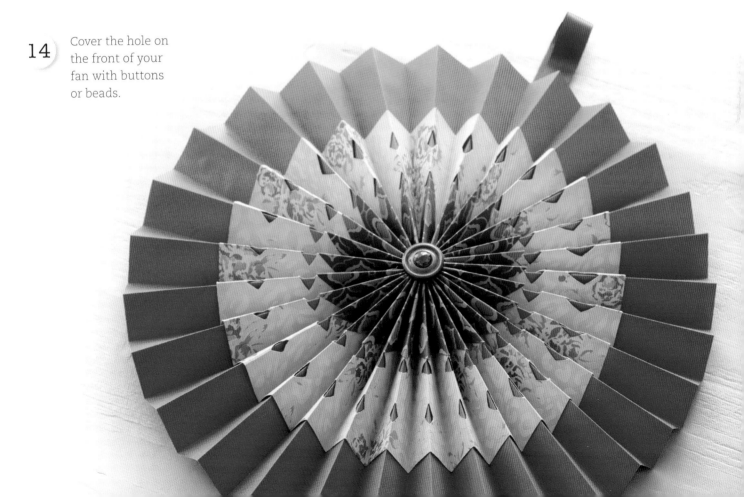

Hanging garlands

Garlands are a simple but effective decoration for any party or celebration. You can use coloured papers that match your theme, but they can also be made from pretty scraps.

Papers

PVA glue and brush

String

Scissors

Beads

Scrap surface

7.5cm (3in) circle punch

Glue stick

You will need

1 Use a punch to cut out circles. You will need six per ball.

2

Fold the circles in half, image sides together.

3 Begin gluing the folded circles on top of each other.

4

Repeat until all the folded circles are glued together.

5

Make two knots on a length of string and glue it between the circles. Close the circles around the string and glue in place.

6

Apply a little glue to the end of the string to stop it from fraying.

7

Thread beads onto the string and make a loop at the end.

Pull the string to close the loop and secure the beads.

8

Repeat the steps to make more balls for your garland.

Snowflake bauble

A simple but pretty winter decoration, these snowflakes can be hung from string or ribbon to great effect. However, they look even better when encased in baubles and placed on a tree.

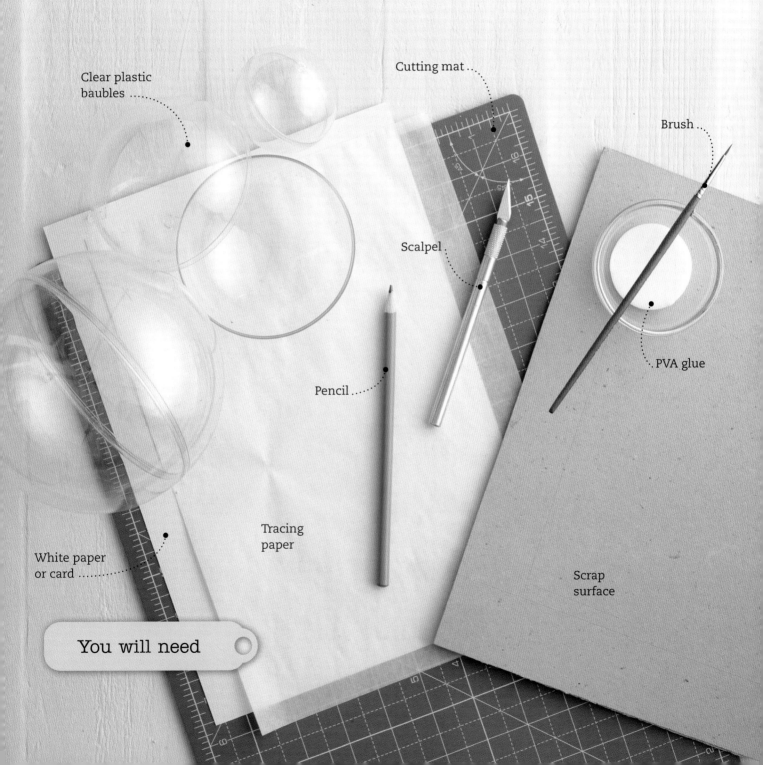

Clear plastic baubles

Cutting mat

Brush

Scalpel

Pencil

PVA glue

White paper or card

Tracing paper

Scrap surface

You will need

1 Trace four templates and place them face down on the paper or card. Rub to transfer.

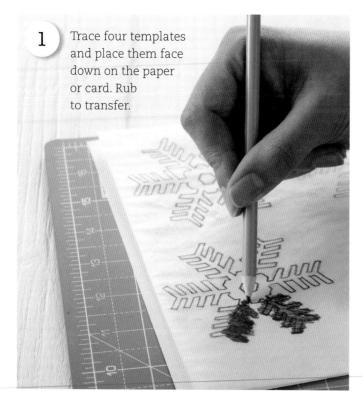

2

Carefully cut out the snowflakes.

3 Fold the snowflakes in half as shown, being careful to align the edges.

4

Apply glue to one side of the folded shape.

Glue one of the shapes to another, then repeat to create a 3D shape.

5

You can scale the template to fit different size baubles, but you may need to glue more snowflakes together to create the same 3D look.

Kids' crafts

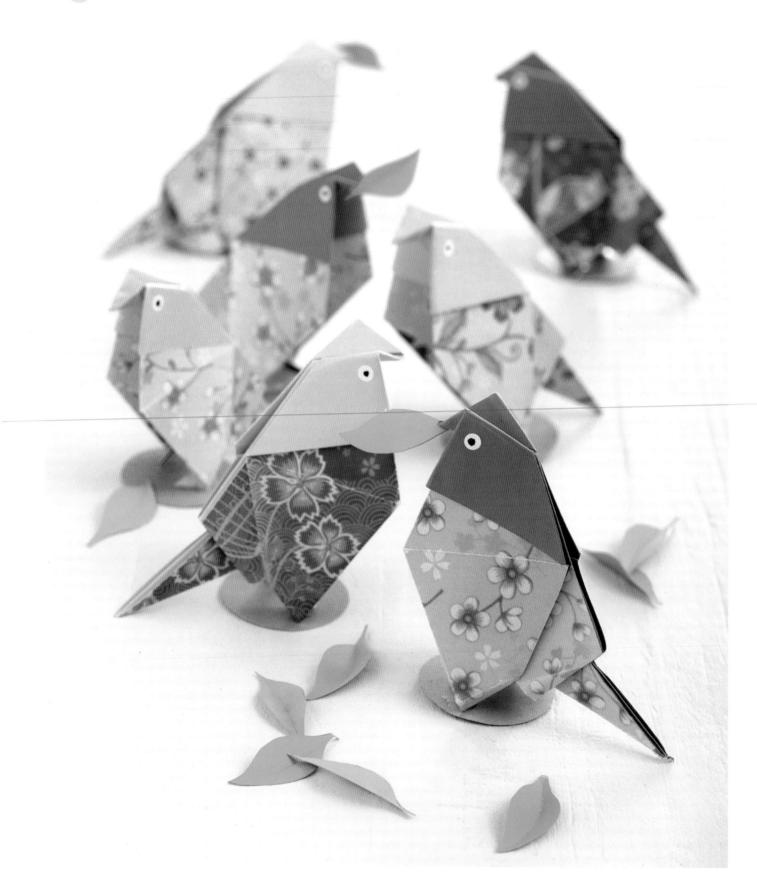

Origami bird

These cute little birds are easy to put together and make great decorations. You can also put paper leaves in their beaks and use them as place holders at a dinner party.

Scalpel

6cm (2½in) circle punch

Cutting mat

Hole punch

Scissors

Hot glue gun and sticks

Squares of paper

Glue

Spray mount

Ruler

You will need

1 Fold the paper in half diagonally.

Open out, then fold two sides in as shown.

2

Turn the paper over and fold the top down.

Turn it back over and fold down the corners.

3

Lift up each flap, pull the top corner to the side, then fold back down as shown.

Tuck the corners underneath so they poke out a little.

4

Fold the bird in half so that the open fold is at the top, then fold the middle in to create a beak.

5

Fold the tail along the top towards the head.

Unfold and refold at the base of the head to create a crease.

6

Open up the tail and fold the bottom section inside using the crease lines as a guide.

7

Cut out a disc of card with a circle punch. Stick the birds feet to the disc using hot glue.

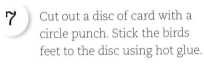

8

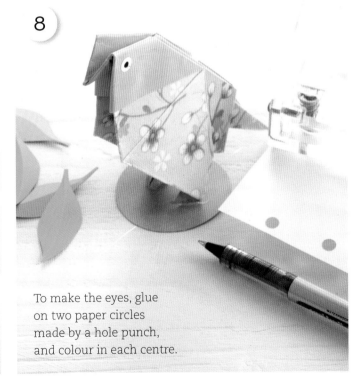

To make the eyes, glue on two paper circles made by a hole punch, and colour in each centre.

Animal mask

Simple to make and fun for kids, you can adapt the basic technique for this bear mask to create a dog, a monkey, or almost any creature.

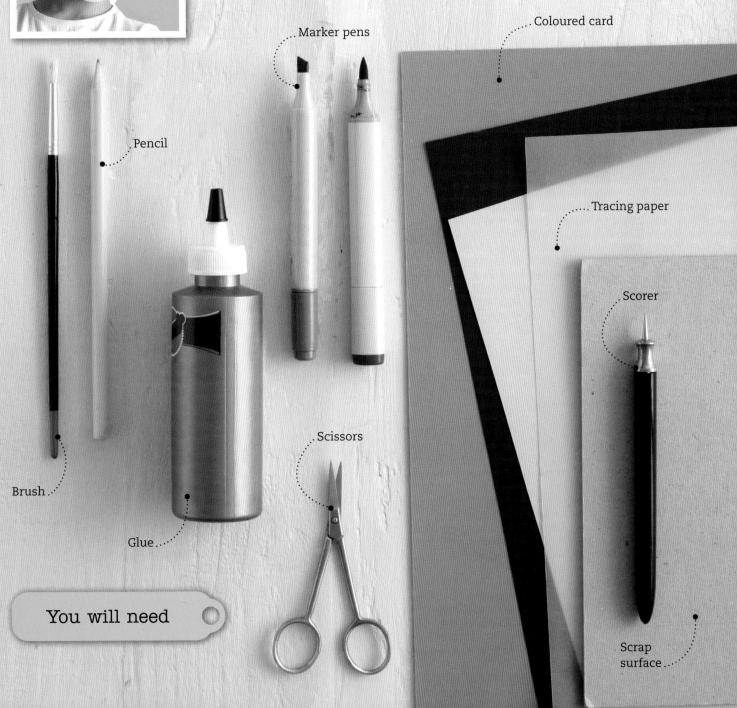

Marker pens

Coloured card

Pencil

Tracing paper

Scorer

Brush

Scissors

Glue

Scrap surface

You will need

1 Cut strips of card and glue them together to make a long, wide band.

Make sure the length matches the circumference of the child's head.

2 Transfer the templates to card using tracing paper.

Fold the paper in half to cut two ears at the same time. Repeat for the inner ears.

3 Stick the ear pieces together and score from the centre of the ear to the bottom.

4 Using the score mark, fold the ear to give it a slightly curved shape. Glue in place.

5

Using the template, cut the patches that go around the eyes.

Measure the distance between the eyes and mark them on the band.

6

Cut out the nose and mouth pieces. Glue together, then stick to the front of the band.

Colour inside the eyes to avoid an orange line when they are cut out.

7

Cut out the eye holes and glue the ears to the back of the mask.

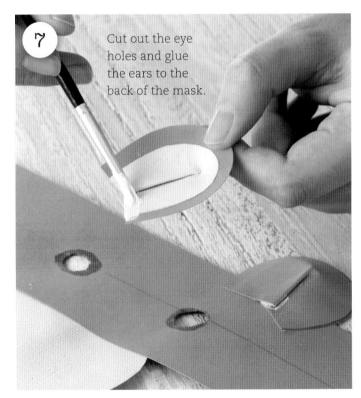

8

Carefully draw around the outside edge of the mouthpiece.

Owl mobile

This cheerful mobile is the perfect decoration to hang above a child's bed. The basic design is fairly easy to adapt, so it's a great project to personalize and give as a gift.

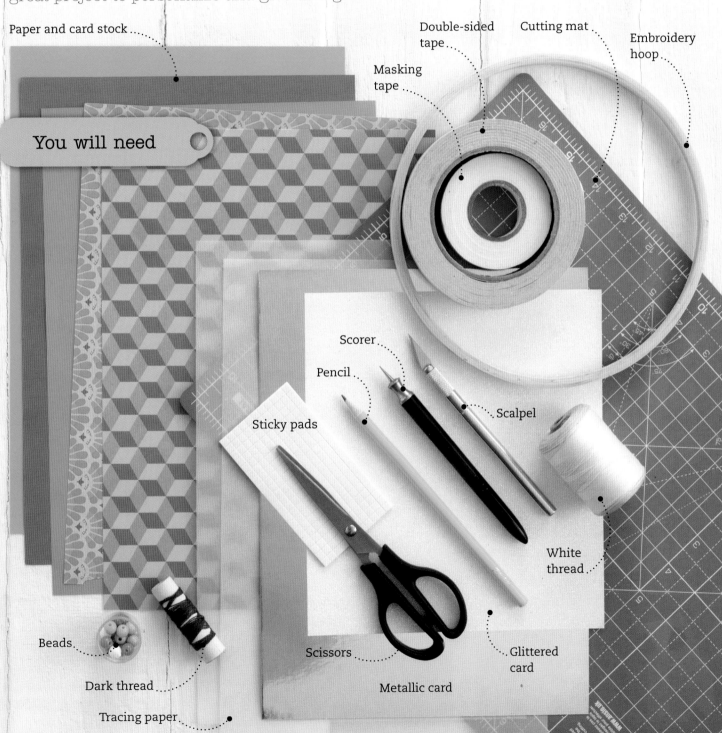

You will need

- Paper and card stock
- Double-sided tape
- Cutting mat
- Embroidery hoop
- Masking tape
- Scorer
- Pencil
- Scalpel
- Sticky pads
- White thread
- Beads
- Scissors
- Glittered card
- Dark thread
- Metallic card
- Tracing paper

Making the owls

1 Fold a sheet of paper in half inward. Trace all the pieces of the template.

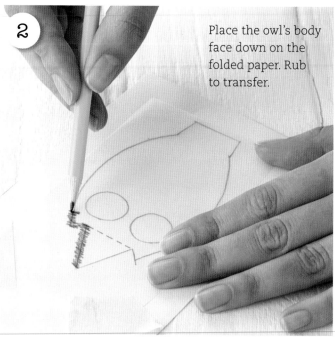

2 Place the owl's body face down on the folded paper. Rub to transfer.

3 Cut out the eyes and bodies to make two halves of your owl.

4 Transfer and cut out all the other template pieces.

5

Cut "U" shapes into the breast to make feathers.

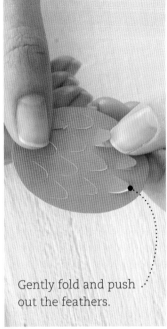

Gently fold and push out the feathers.

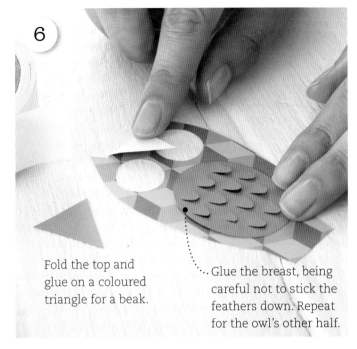

6

Fold the top and glue on a coloured triangle for a beak.

Glue the breast, being careful not to stick the feathers down. Repeat for the owl's other half.

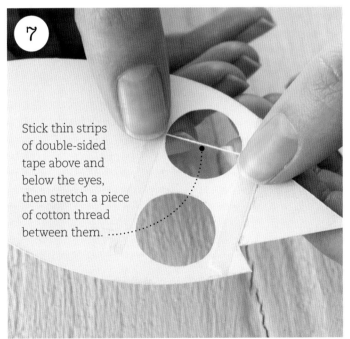

7

Stick thin strips of double-sided tape above and below the eyes, then stretch a piece of cotton thread between them.

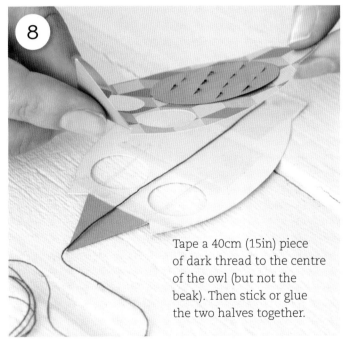

8

Tape a 40cm (15in) piece of dark thread to the centre of the owl (but not the beak). Then stick or glue the two halves together.

9 Use double-sided tape or glue to attach the wings to the body.

10 Cut four circles and glue to either side of the thread between the eyes. Secure the beak with a sticky pad.

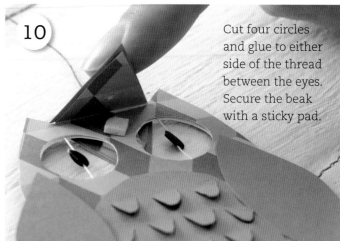

11 Roll a piece of paper around a pencil and glue to make a branch. Remove the pencil.

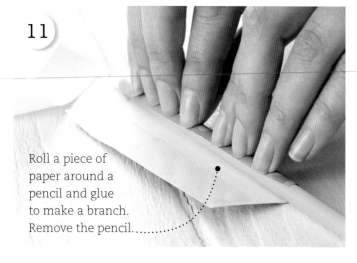

12 Attach leaves with tape or glue.

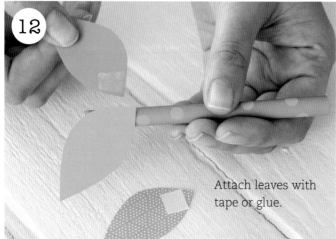

13 Cut a slot in the branch for the owl and glue it in place. Repeat to make the other four owls.

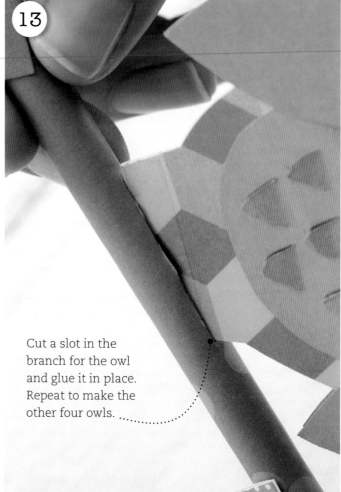

Assembling the mobile

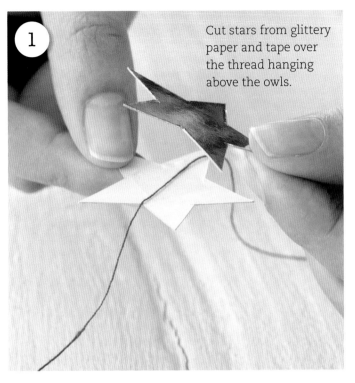

1 Cut stars from glittery paper and tape over the thread hanging above the owls.

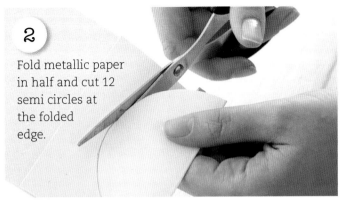

2 Fold metallic paper in half and cut 12 semi circles at the folded edge.

Stick the folded circles on top of each other.

3 Tie a bead to a piece of thread and place it in the seam between the circles.

Stick the final pieces of the circle together to form a ball.

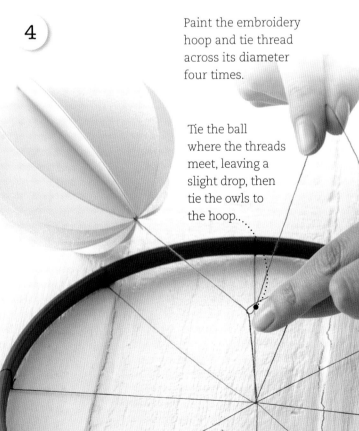

4 Paint the embroidery hoop and tie thread across its diameter four times.

Tie the ball where the threads meet, leaving a slight drop, then tie the owls to the hoop.

Party crown

Fun and diverse, paper crowns can be made to suit any dressing up costume or party theme. Try adapting the basic template to create your own designs.

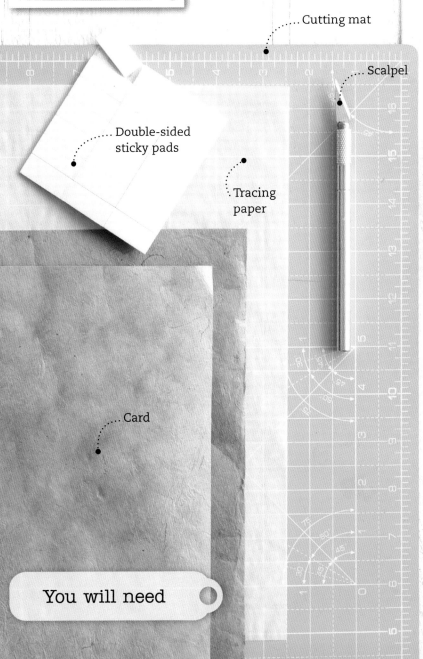

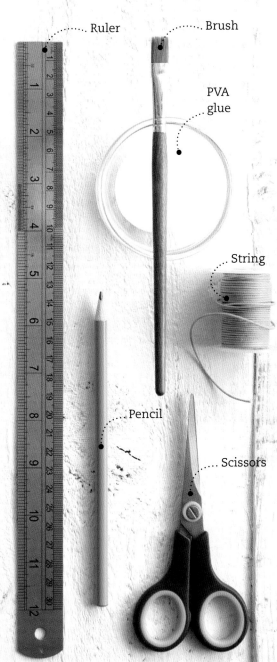

Cutting mat

Scalpel

Double-sided sticky pads

Tracing paper

Card

Ruler

Brush

PVA glue

String

Pencil

Scissors

You will need

1 Trace the templates and lay them face down on card. Rub with a pencil to transfer the image.

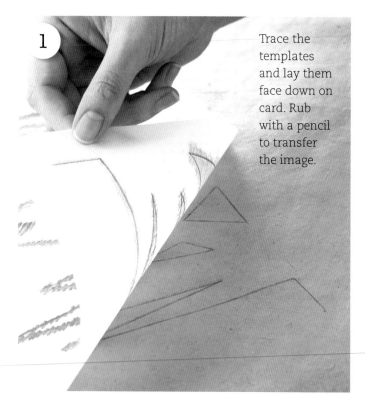

2 Cut out the shapes with a scalpel, using a ruler to make sure the cuts are straight.

3 Apply glue to the points of the crown.

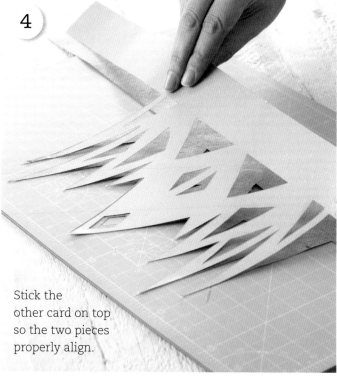

4 Stick the other card on top so the two pieces properly align.

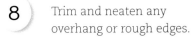

5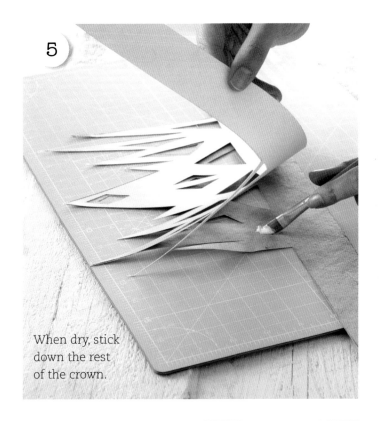

When dry, stick down the rest of the crown.

6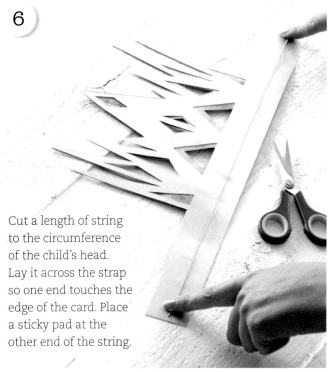

Cut a length of string to the circumference of the child's head. Lay it across the strap so one end touches the edge of the card. Place a sticky pad at the other end of the string.

7

Peel the back off the sticky pad and stick down the strap.

8

Trim and neaten any overhang or rough edges.

Flowers

Cherry blossom

Though most popular in Japan, cherry blossoms are a symbol of renewal and growth the world over. This gorgeous paper version will make you feel like spring is always just around the corner.

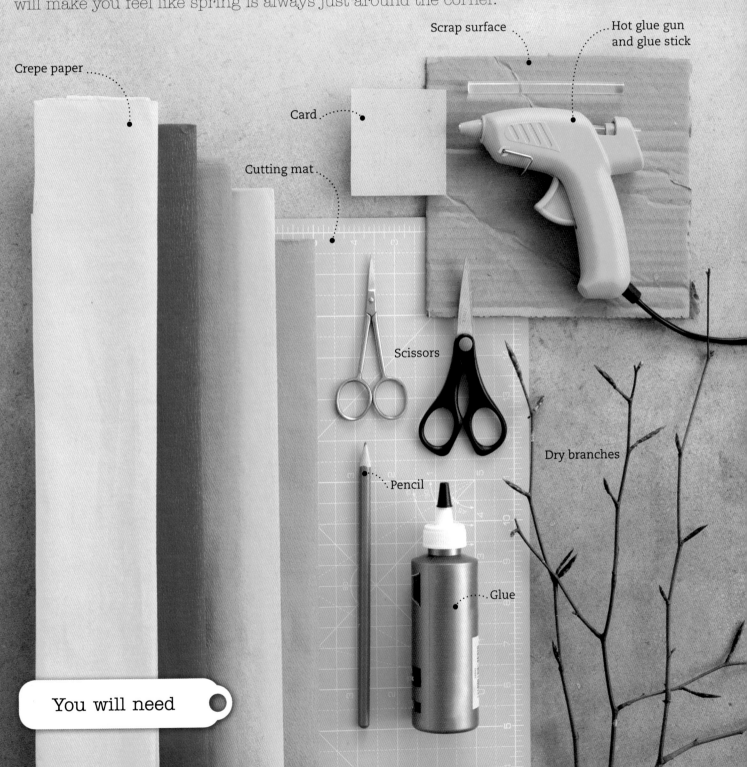

Crepe paper

Scrap surface

Hot glue gun and glue stick

Card

Cutting mat

Scissors

Dry branches

Pencil

Glue

You will need

1 Trace the templates and place upside down on card. Rub with a pencil to transfer.

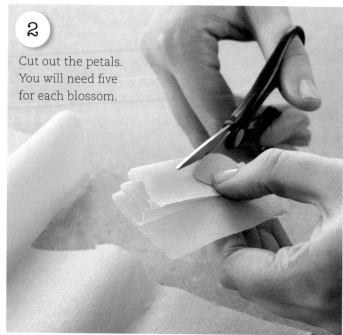

2 Cut out the petals. You will need five for each blossom.

3 Gently stretch the centre papers between your fingers.

4 Fringe the centre papers finely, about 1cm (½in) deep.

Roll the centres between your fingers and glue the opposite ends.

5 Cup the petals between your fingers to shape them.

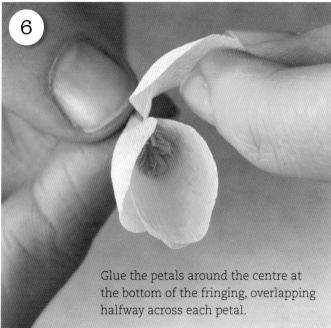

6 Glue the petals around the centre at the bottom of the fringing, overlapping halfway across each petal.

7 Once dry, cut the stems to 0.5cm (¼in).

Gently squeeze the petals down to form the blossom.

8 Hot glue onto the branch at the point you wish. Try gluing the blossoms in clusters for a realistic look.

Peony

Prized for their size and petal count, peonies are one of the most popular flowers in the world. And while paper versions can't replicate their scent, they definitely deliver the wow factor.

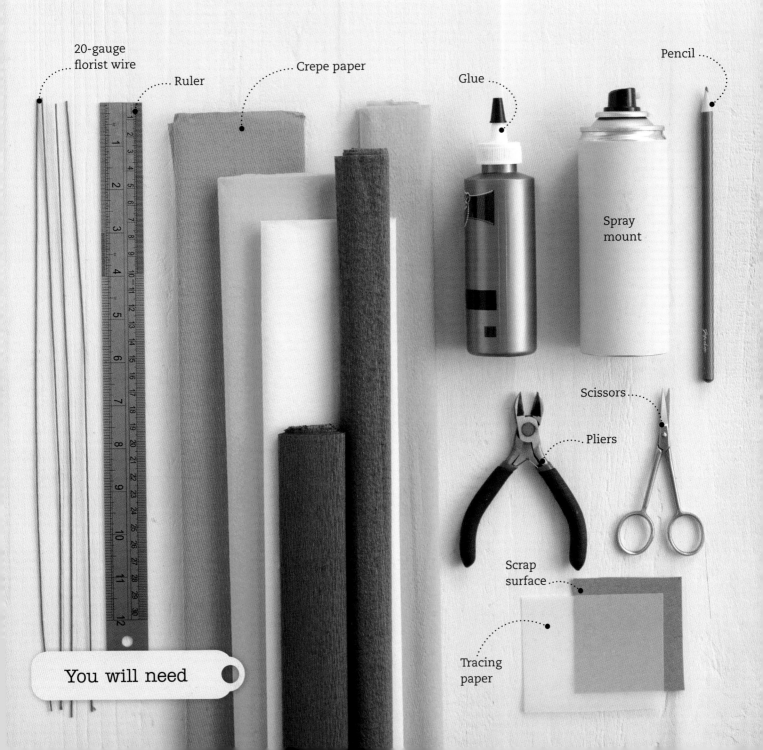

20-gauge florist wire

Ruler

Crepe paper

Glue

Spray mount

Pencil

Scissors

Pliers

Scrap surface

Tracing paper

You will need

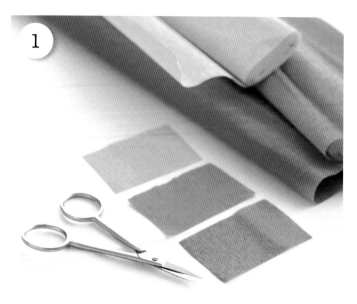

1

Cut three different-coloured 6x4cm (2½x1½in) sheets of crepe paper and stack on top of each other.

2

Fringe about halfway through the paper and crumple the ends.

Place florist wire at one end and add glue. Roll the paper around the wire.

3

Cut seven petals from the small template and cup them gently with your thumbs. Glue around the centre, overlapping each time.

4

Cut and cup eight petals from the larger template and glue to the flower.

Cut and glue three green pieces of paper at the bottom for the calyx.

Wrap a long strip of green paper diagonally around the wire.

Wrap a 1cm (½in) strip of paper around a second piece of florist wire, gluing on leaves as you go.

Glue the two pieces of wire together and wrap with more paper to secure.

Ranunculus

Known for their delicate petals and brilliant colours, a ranunculus arrangement can breathe life into any room. This simple and beautiful paper version is no exception.

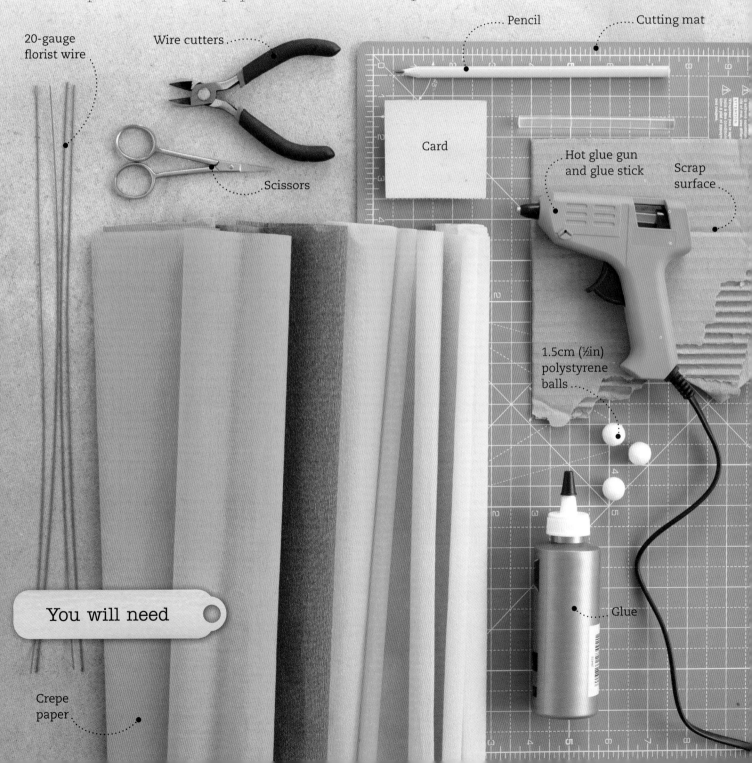

20-gauge florist wire

Wire cutters

Pencil

Cutting mat

Card

Scissors

Hot glue gun and glue stick

Scrap surface

1.5cm (½in) polystyrene balls

Glue

You will need

Crepe paper

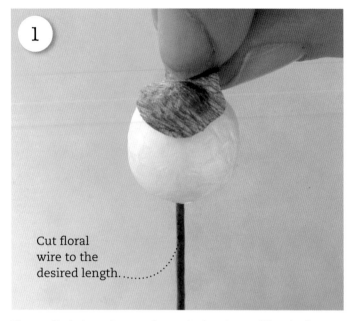

Place a little hot glue on the end of a piece of floral wire and insert it into the centre of a polystyrene ball. Glue a small dark green circle on top of the ball, then cut out 15 light green petals using template 1.

Cut floral wire to the desired length.

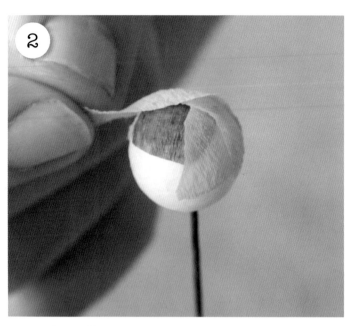

Cup each petal between your thumb and forefinger and apply glue to the bottom. Glue a petal so the curved edge almost meets the centre of the ball then overlap five more by 50 percent so they curve away from the one before.

Add the remaining green petals, but layer them slightly higher than before. Cut out and cup 11 yellow petals from the same template and overlap these on top of the green petals, bringing them slightly higher.

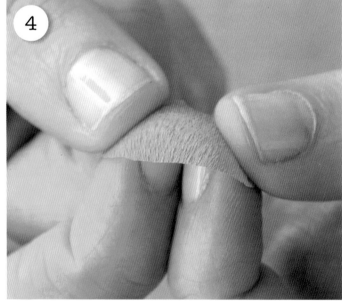

Cut out the orange petals. You will need 21 from template 2 and 18 from template 3. These petals need to have a deeper cup than the yellow or green ones.

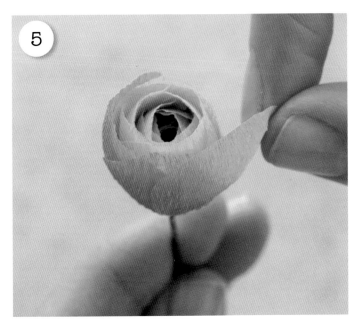

Add a little glue to the bottom of the petals from template 2 and begin gluing them to the flower slightly higher than the yellow layer. Continue overlapping as you go, bringing the layers down slightly as the flower begins to take shape.

Glue the petals from template 3 so that the base of each petal touches the stem and covers any remaining areas of the polystyrene ball. Continue overlapping these petals around the flower.

To make the calyx, cut four green pieces of crepe paper and slightly cup in the middle to give them a little shape. Glue the end of the calyx shapes to the foot of the stem.

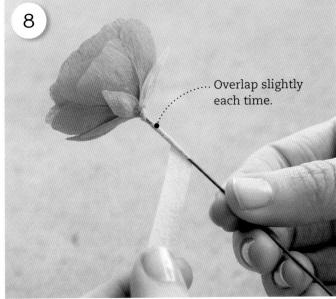

Overlap slightly each time.

Cut a strip of paper across the grain about 1cm wide and stretch it out. Glue one end under the calyx and wind the paper around the wire, applying a little glue every six or so turns. Repeat until the stem is your desired thickness.

Daisy

These bright and cheerful daisies add a touch of spring to any room. Although they are made of paper, their white petals and yellow centres manage to look quite realistic.

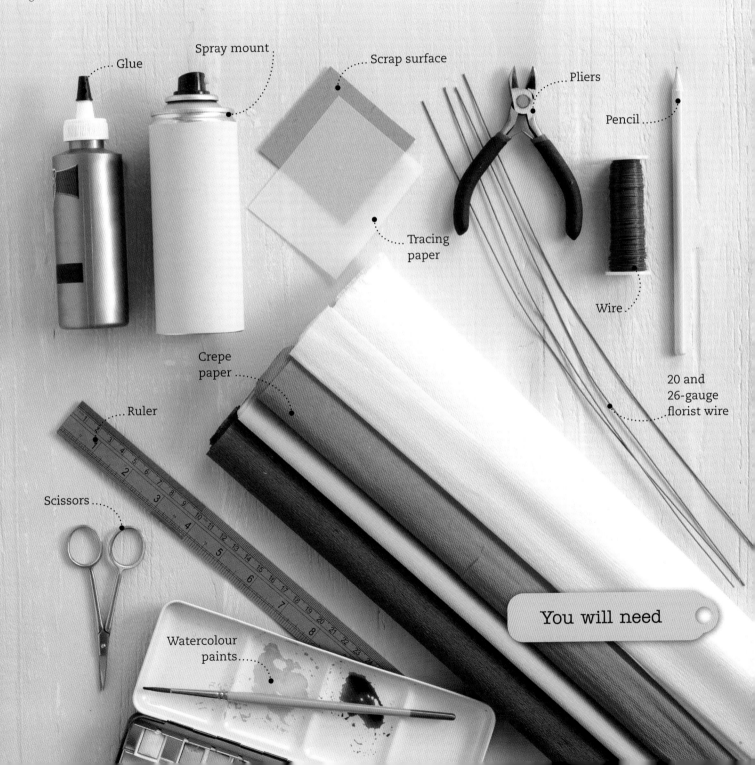

Glue

Spray mount

Scrap surface

Pliers

Pencil

Tracing paper

Wire

Crepe paper

20 and 26-gauge florist wire

Ruler

Scissors

Watercolour paints

You will need

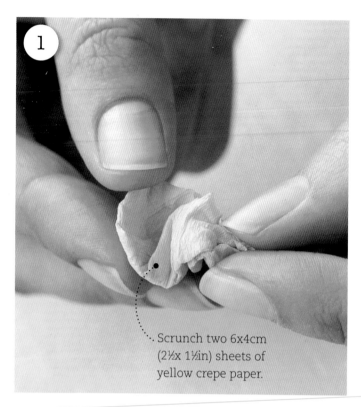

1 Scrunch two 6x4cm (2½x 1½in) sheets of yellow crepe paper.

2 Push florist wire into the paper and glue another square of crepe paper around it.

Squeeze until it holds its shape.

3 Cut a 11x5cm (4¼x2¼in) piece of white crepe paper. Hold in half and cut into petal shapes.

4 Wrap the petals around the centre of the flower.

Bind to the stem with 26-gauge wire. Use pliers if you have trouble keeping it tight.

5 Use the dull side of a pair of scissors to curl the petals into a realistic shape.

6 Trim away the excess yellow paper at the top of the stem.

7 Wind a 1cm (½in) strip of crepe paper around the wire a few times. Cut leaves and glue to the wire, then wrap another green strip around to secure.

8 Paint around the centre with yellow watercolour paint.

Anemone

You can make amazing paper anemones in a variety of shades, from pale pink and lilac to a rich jewel-like purple. Their delicate crepe paper petals are almost impossible to distinguish from the real thing.

Wire

Brush

Pencil

Watercolour

Scissors

Pliers

Scrap surface

Tracing paper

Crepe paper

20-gauge florist wire

Spray mount

Glue

You will need

Ruler

Cut two squares of black crepe paper, then cut one in half. Stretch out the square, then scrunch one of the rectangles into a ball and wrap the other rectangle around it.

Hold in place until dry.

Place the ball of crepe paper in the middle of the stretched square and dot small amounts of glue around it. Holding the centre down with straight floral wire, pull the corners of the square up around the scrunched paper and wire.

Cut a strip of purple crepe paper about 5cm (2in) long and fringe two-thirds of it. Wrap it around the black centre and glue in place, then secure with wire and paint the tips black.

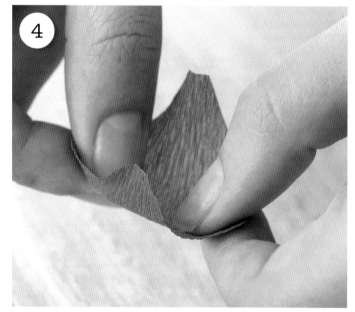

Using the template, cut six petal shapes from the purple crepe paper. Push your thumbs into the centre and gently stretch outwards to give them a rounded shape.

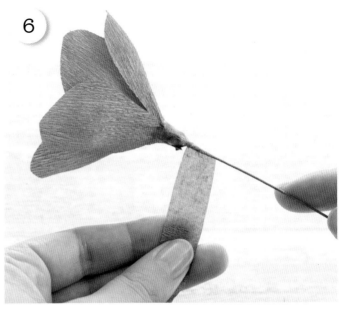

Dab glue around the base of the cut petals and attach them to the stalk, overlapping slightly. Once the glue has dried, cut away the excess black crepe paper below the petals.

Wrap the base of the flower with a long strip of green crepe paper and then wrap it down the stem diagonally. Glue in place at the bottom. Repeat until the stem is thick enough.

Use the template to cut four leaves from green crepe paper. Curl the leaves with scissors to give them a realistic shape, then glue them to the stem underneath the flower.

Finally, gently curl the tips of the petals over the scissors so that they curve inwards.

Daffodil

These bright and cheerful daffodils are simple to make and will last a lot longer than the real thing. With their natural looking yellow petals, you can imagine it's spring all-year long!

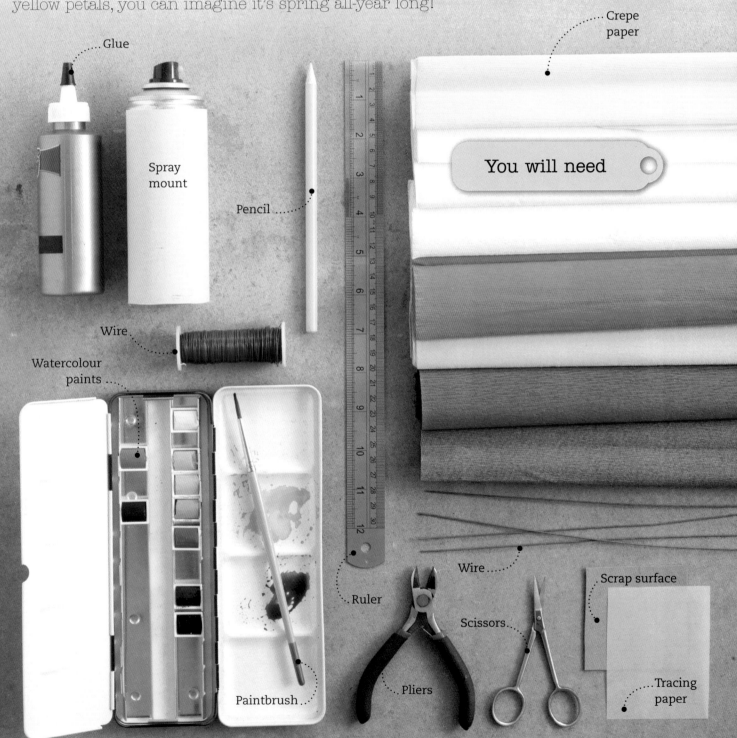

Glue

Spray mount

Pencil

Wire

Watercolour paints

Crepe paper

You will need

Ruler

Wire

Scrap surface

Paintbrush

Pliers

Scissors

Tracing paper

1 Place florist's wire at one end of a small piece of fringed crepe paper. Add glue and roll the paper around the wire.

2 Cut orange paper for the trumpet and brush the edge with red paint.

Once dry, wrap the trumpet around the stamens and secure with wire.

3 Lightly spray some spray mount over a sheet of crepe paper. Cut out six petals for each flower.

4 Pinch the top of the petal until it forms a realistic shape.

Shape the petals with your thumbs.

5 With your finger and thumb, gently stretch the trumpet part of the flower.

6 Arrange the petals around the stem. Wrap strips of green paper diagonally around the stem to hold in place.

7 Add some green leaves to the stem; glue and hold in place with strips of paper.

8 Glue between the trumpet and the petals.

Squeeze gently into shape.

Large rose

Perfect for a wedding or birthday party, these giant roses will create a real talking point. The dramatic and delicate petals makes them look stunning and appealing.

You will need

Crepe paper and cardboard

Dowelling rod

Round pencil

Stem tape

Scissors

Hot glue gun and sticks

Strong florist wire

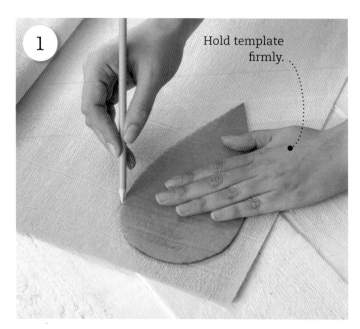

Hold template firmly.

Copy the templates to cardboard and cut them out. Draw around them and cut out six small, ten medium, and six large petals from pink crepe paper. Then cut eight sepals and one large leaf from dark green crepe paper.

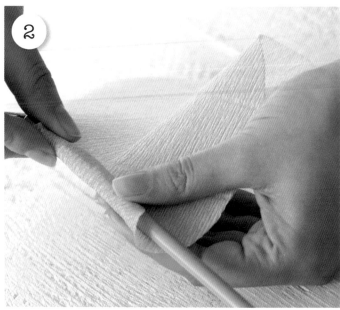

Put two small petals to one side, then use a pencil to curl the tips of the remaining petals. Stretch the paper slightly as you roll it. For the large petals, roll each lobe separately.

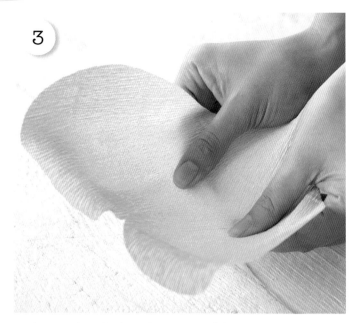

Push your thumbs into the centre of the small petals to cup them. Push out the medium and large petals in the same way, but this time at three points on the petal.

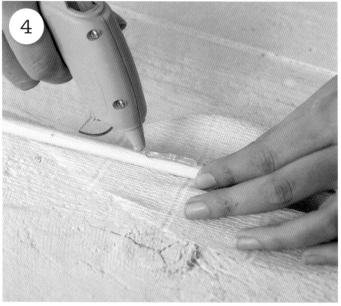

Add a dab of hot glue to the bottom point of the two small, uncurled petals and attach them to the dowelling. Apply glue to the top of the rod and roll the petals into a spiral around it.

Going from small to large, attach the remaining petals in the same way, spacing by eye. Add glue further up the petal to keep the shape if need be. You also may have to stretch the base of the large petals to fit.

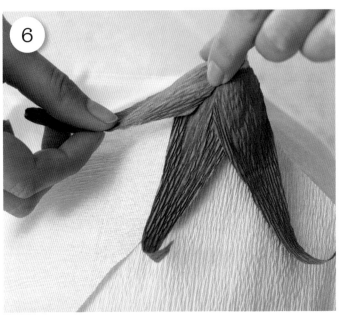

For the sepals, slightly stretch the bottom of each one so that they fit around the base of the flower head. Then curl the points and glue them on, ensuring that some of the paper attaches to the dowelling.

Place a line of hot glue along the centre of the large green leaf and attach the floral wire. Fold the leaf in half and allow the hot glue to set before opening again.

Starting at the base of the rose, wind the stem tape around the dowelling. After a few turns, add the wired leaf, and glue it in place with the glue gun. Continue to wrap the stem tape around the dowelling until you reach the end.

Kusudama

These beautiful origami flowers are surprisingly simple to make and will liven up any room. They sit perfectly in a vase, but you can stick them to almost anything with a little glue.

You will need

Squares of paper

Glue

1

Choose your paper colour. You'll need five squares per flower.

2

Fold into a triangle.

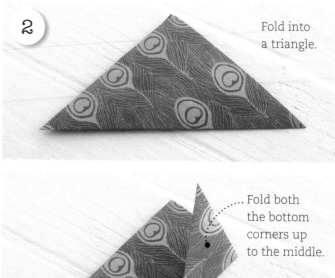

Fold both the bottom corners up to the middle.

3

Fold the points back so they line up with the outside edges.

4

Poke a finger inside each flap to pop them out, then flatten along the seam to create two kite shapes.

5) Fold the top triangle of the kite shapes flat so they are level with the long edge behind.

6) Fold the sides in to create a square shape.

7) Bring the two sides together to create a petal. Glue in place.

8) Repeat until you have five petals, then glue them together along the join one at a time.

Wreath

Making a wreath is a great way to bring together all the flowers you have created into a single display. Try different combinations to get the effect that suits your home.

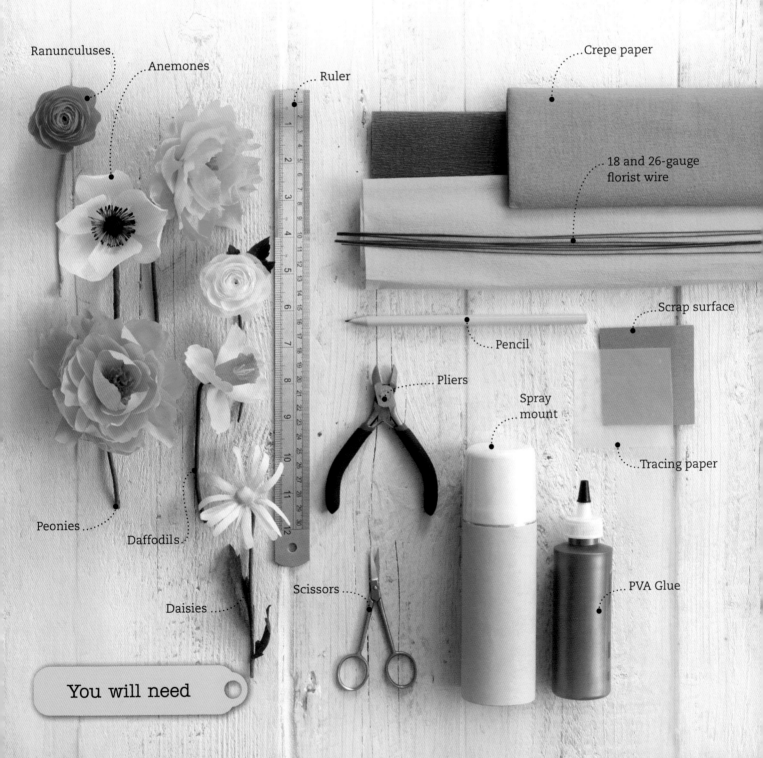

Ranunculuses.

Anemones

Ruler

Crepe paper

18 and 26-gauge florist wire

Scrap surface

Pencil

Pliers

Spray mount

Tracing paper

Peonies

Daffodils

PVA Glue

Daisies

Scissors

You will need

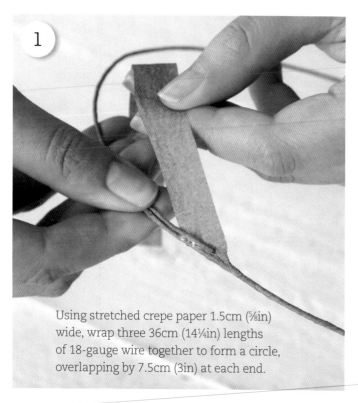

1 Using stretched crepe paper 1.5cm (⅝in) wide, wrap three 36cm (14¼in) lengths of 18-gauge wire together to form a circle, overlapping by 7.5cm (3in) at each end.

2 Spray mount two shades of green crepe together and cut out around 60 leaves using the template.

3 Pinch the bottom of the leaves to make a realistic shape.

4 Crowd some sections and leave others sparse.

Wrap another three lengths of wire together as before, but don't complete the circle. Tuck leaves into the wire as you wrap it.

5

Attach the end of the leafed ring to the original circle using the 26-gauge wire.

6

Bend the leafed ring around the original circle, attaching it at various points using 26-gauge wire.

7 Use 26-gauge wire to attach flowers to the wreath.

8

Start with the larger flowers and add smaller ones around them.

Buttonhole

For a wedding or other special event, buttonholes add to the sense of occasion. If you make them from paper, you can prepare them well ahead of time and be sure they'll still look fresh on the big day.

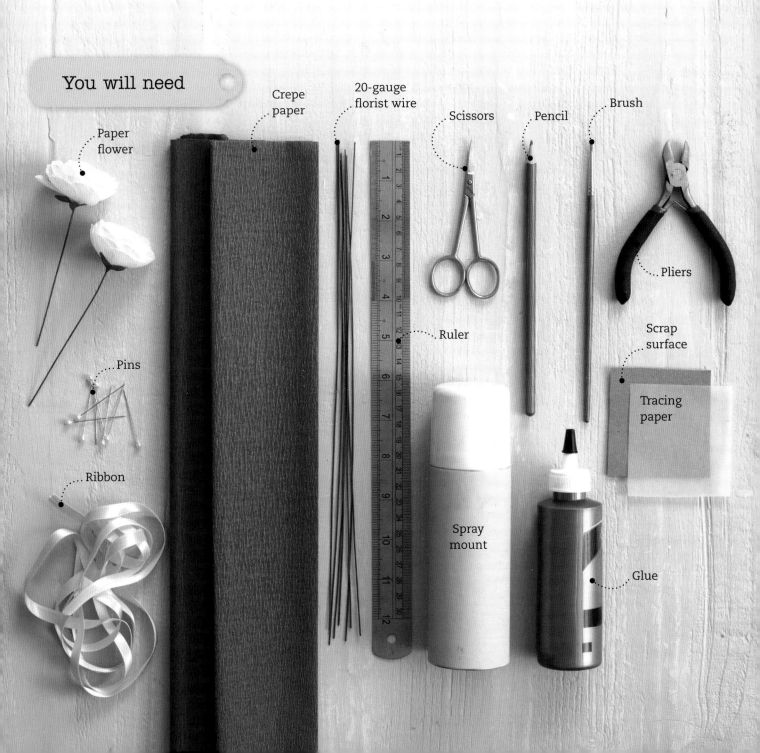

You will need

Paper flower

Crepe paper

20-gauge florist wire

Scissors

Pencil

Brush

Pliers

Ruler

Scrap surface

Tracing paper

Pins

Ribbon

Spray mount

Glue

1 Cut three leaves from green crepe paper and snip the edges to create a serrated effect.

2 Wrap the base of the leaves around the end of a length of floral wire and glue in place.

3 Position the leaves at the base of the flower's head. Hold both wires together, and wrap them with a long strip of green crepe paper.

4 Cut the stem about 4cm (1½in) from the flower head using pliers.

5

Wrap green paper around the end of the stem to neaten.

6

Tie a length of ribbon around the top of the stem.

7

Wrap the ribbon around the stem from top to bottom, then wrap it back up to the top.

8

Tie off again at the base of the flower head and cut away excess ribbon.

Large poppy

Guaranteed to make an impression, this giant poppy is a real show stopper. It would make an excellent decoration for a festival, party, child's room, or a wedding.

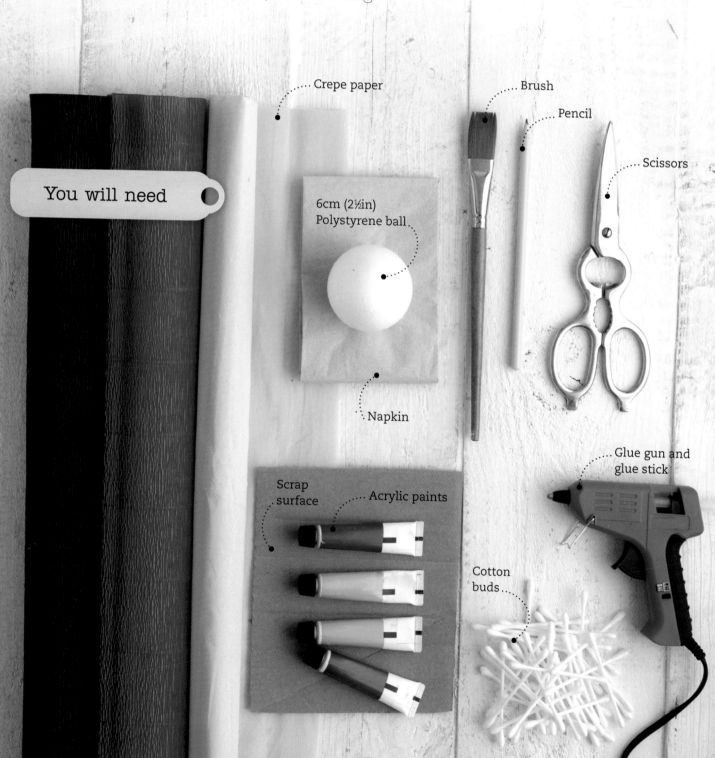

Crepe paper

Brush

Pencil

Scissors

You will need

6cm (2½in) Polystyrene ball

Napkin

Glue gun and glue stick

Scrap surface

Acrylic paints

Cotton buds

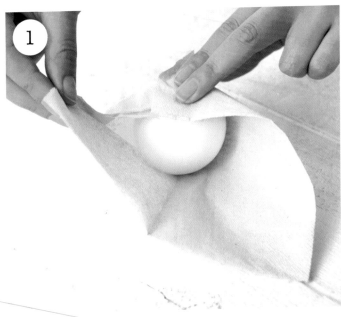

Wrap a napkin or square of beige tissue paper around the polystyrene ball so that it is completely covered. Use a glue gun to secure it in place.

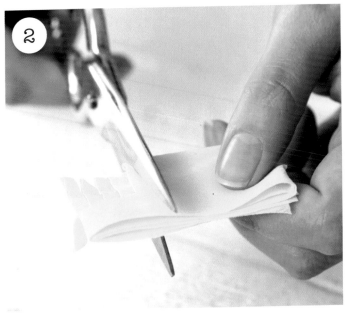

Cut a strip of yellow tissue paper slightly longer than the ball's circumference and 8cm (3in) wide. Fold it up and cut halfway into it from one side to create a fringed effect. Wrap around the ball and secure with the glue gun.

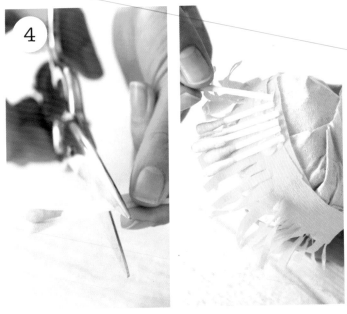

Mix your paint and slightly dilute it with water (you will need a mix of green and yellow buds). Dip the buds in the paint to colour them, then remove and set aside to dry.

Once dry, cut the yellow cotton buds in half and stick them around the ball with a glue gun. Don't worry about making them perfect, you want them to look a little uneven.

5

Cut some black tissue paper as in Step 2, although this time it should be longer – in line with the wider circumference of the ball – and 10cm (4in) wide. Attach with hot glue.

6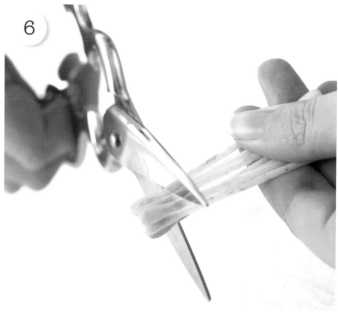

The green cotton buds for the stamens need to be a little longer, so instead of cutting them in half, cut the tips off of one end.

7

Glue the green buds around the outside of the ball so they fan out. You may find it easier to do this by attaching them lower on the ball.

Transfer the petal templates onto cardboard and cut them out. Draw around the templates onto the crepe paper, then cut out three small and three large petals.

Shape the top of the petals by twisting and stretching the paper. To achieve the petals' overall shape, work into the centre of the petals with your thumbs to create curves.

Glue the small petals to the centre of the flower, ensuring they are evenly spaced. Try to shape them to the curve of the ball as you stick them.

Shape the centres of the large petals in the same manner used for the small. Attach to the rest of the flower head, placing these petals in the gaps between the smaller petals.

12 Finally, carefully crumple the petals inwards with your hands so that the ends curve into the centre of the flower.

Festival headband

While primarily worn at festivals, these headbands have become increasingly popular at weddings and springtime events. Most combinations of bright flowers will work well.

You will need

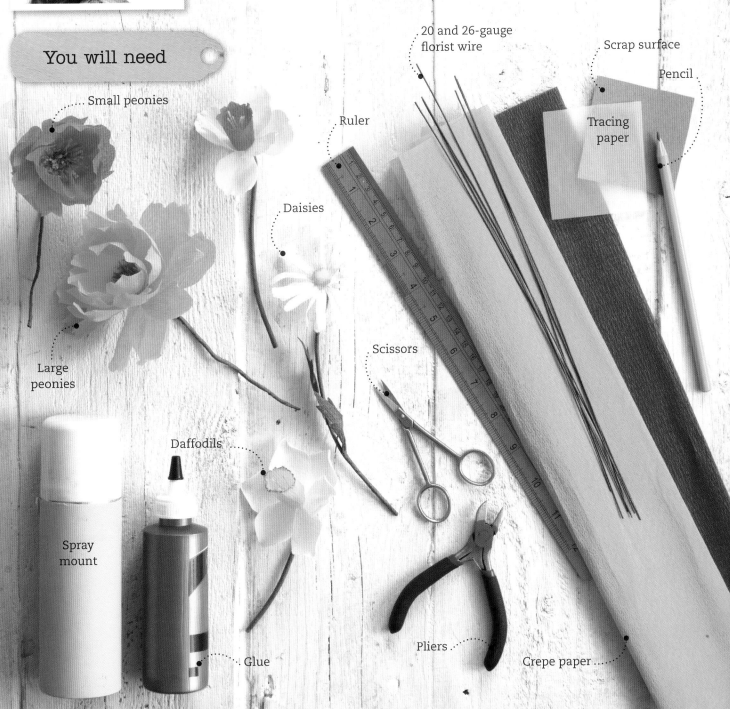

Small peonies

Large peonies

Daisies

Daffodils

Ruler

Scissors

20 and 26-gauge florist wire

Scrap surface

Pencil

Tracing paper

Spray mount

Glue

Pliers

Crepe paper

1

Wrap two 36cm (14¼in) strips of 20-gauge wire in 1.5cm (⅝in) wide crepe paper, overlapping the ends of the wire by 7.5cm (3in).

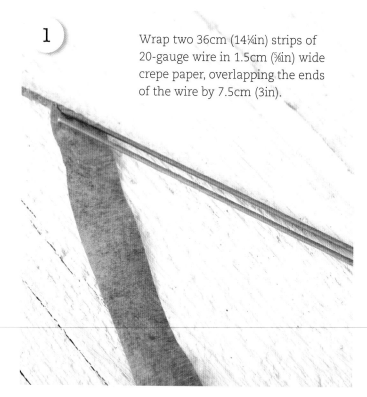

2

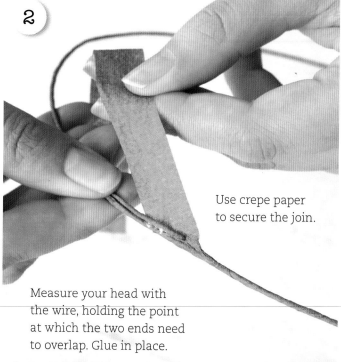

Use crepe paper to secure the join.

Measure your head with the wire, holding the point at which the two ends need to overlap. Glue in place.

3

Spray mount two shades of green crepe paper together. Cut out 25 leaves and pinch to shape.

4

Make five stems with five leaves on each.

Wrap a 6cm (2½in) length of 20-gauge wire with a 1.5cm (⅝in) wide strip of crepe paper, tucking and gluing in the leaves between wraps.

5

Attach the leaf stems to the ring using 26-gauge wire. Keep the ends of the wire away from the inside of the ring. Trim the stems if necessary.

6

Space the leaves out evenly, facing towards a focal point at the front of the ring. Leave a large gap at the back.

7

Attach the flowers using 26-gauge wire. Place a large peony at the focal point and space the other flowers around the headband.

8

Wrap the ring of wire in strips of green crepe paper. This will cover up any bits of wire and strengthen the ring.

Scrapbooking

Edge punch

Paper

Making a scrapbook

Scrapbooks provide the perfect home for your photographs, letters, tickets, postcards, newspaper clippings, maps, gift tags, or anything else you find meaningful. The basic steps are simple: choose a theme and fill the book with mementos. After that it's just a matter of adding embellishments and decorations to make them your own.

The beauty of scrapbooks is that they feel truly personal to you. Whilst popular themes include weddings, family history, travel, or a baby's first year, you can make them for just about anything you treasure.

The following pages cover some of the basic tools and know-how you'll need to get you started, but the secret to making the perfect scrapbook is simple – fill them with the things that mean the most to you.

Paper punch

Spiral-bound
scrapbook or album

Glue dot
applicator

Foam pads

Paper tape

Bone folder

Assorted card

Edging
scissors

Patterned envelope

Photo corners and frames

Make your favourite photos look even more special by adding corners and frames. These steps can be adapted to fit photos of any size in your collection.

You will need

- Patterned paper
- Scissors
- Tape
- White paper
- Ruler
- Scalpel

Photo corners

1 Cut a short strip of paper and fold one leg at a right angle at the centre.

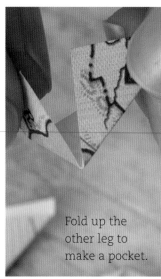

Fold up the other leg to make a pocket.

2 Trim any excess and slip a corner of your photo into each pocket. Tape to secure.

Retro photo frames

1 Transfer the template to paper and cut out with a ruler and scalpel.

Lay your photo face down and place tape around the back edges.

2 Turn the photo right side up and lay the frame over top.

Bunting and bows

If there is a lot of blank space left on your pages, try adding decorative elements such as bunting, ribbon, or these little paper bows. They can help to fill the space without making your pages look too cluttered.

You will need

• Coloured paper
• Scissors
• Double-sided tape
• String
• Origami paper

Bunting

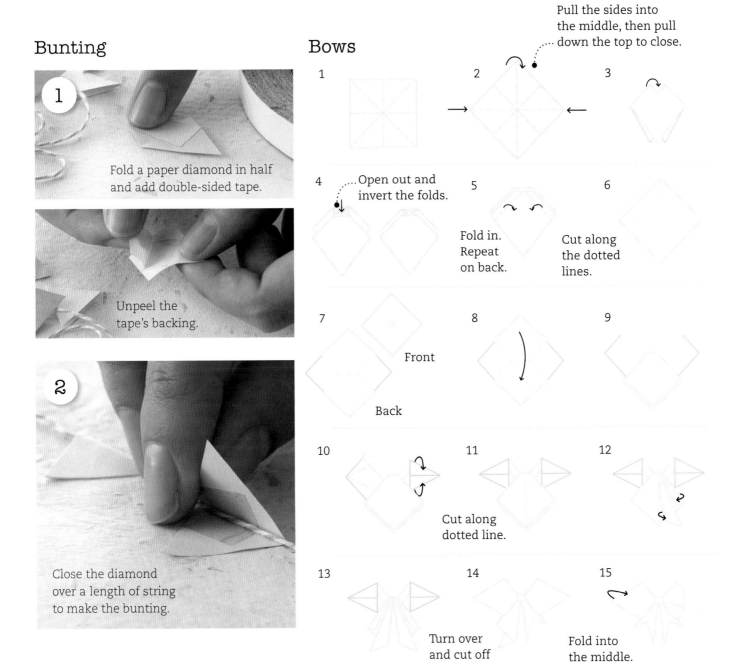

1 Fold a paper diamond in half and add double-sided tape.

Unpeel the tape's backing.

2 Close the diamond over a length of string to make the bunting.

Bows

1

2 Pull the sides into the middle, then pull down the top to close.

3

4 Open out and invert the folds.

5 Fold in. Repeat on back.

6 Cut along the dotted lines.

7 Front / Back

8

9

10

11 Cut along dotted line.

12

13

14 Turn over and cut off the ends.

15 Fold into the middle.

Storage pockets

If you're looking to store items in your scrapbook without having to stick them directly onto the pages, create these storage pockets from paper. They're perfect for holding little mementos, and can be made in a range of shapes.

You will need

- Paper
- Scissors
- Glue or double-sided tape

Heart box

1 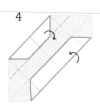 Turn the paper over.

2   3

4  5   6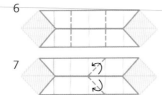

7

8 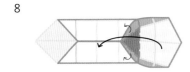 9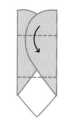

10 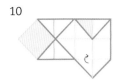 11   12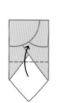

Repeat steps 8–12 on the other side.

13   14

Envelopes

1  2

Apply glue or tape here.

3 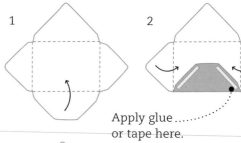 4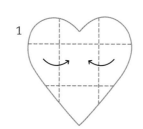

Heart envelopes

1 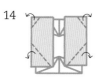 2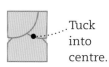

3   4

Tuck into centre.

Rosettes

Simple but eye-catching, rosettes are a great way to adorn your pages and add a little extra charm. The accordion fold used to make them can be used to make embellishments such as to a pram or crib, but what you do with them is up to you.

Basic rosette

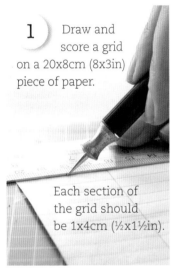

1 Draw and score a grid on a 20x8cm (8x3in) piece of paper.

Each section of the grid should be 1x4cm (½x1½in).

Cut the paper in half lengthwise, then fold each scored line like an accordion.

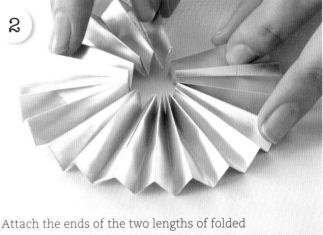

2

Attach the ends of the two lengths of folded paper with double-sided tape to form a circle.

Pram

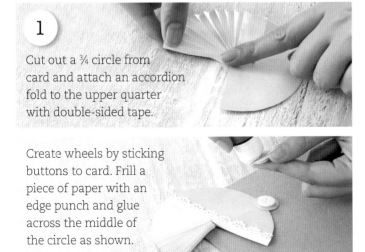

1 Cut out a ¾ circle from card and attach an accordion fold to the upper quarter with double-sided tape.

Create wheels by sticking buttons to card. Frill a piece of paper with an edge punch and glue across the middle of the circle as shown.

2

Tie a short piece of ribbon into a bow and stick it on for an extra flourish.

Gilding and embossing

Add an extra dimension to your embellishments by gilding or embossing them. We've gilded a doily and embossed a heart, but these techniques are easily adaptable.

You will need

- Doilies
- Tracing paper
- Pencil
- Scissors
- Tape
- Gold spray paint
- Cardboard
- Card
- Scrap surface
- Scalpel
- Bone folder

Gilding

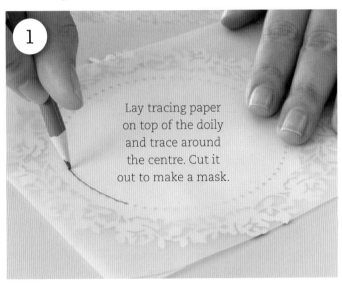

1 Lay tracing paper on top of the doily and trace around the centre. Cut it out to make a mask.

2 Tape the mask to the doily and spray everything gold. Remove the mask and discard.

Embossing

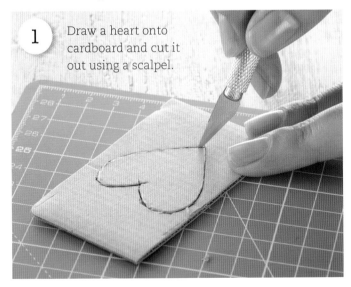

1 Draw a heart onto cardboard and cut it out using a scalpel.

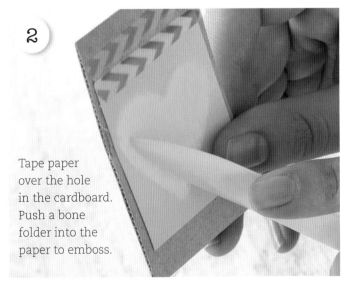

2 Tape paper over the hole in the cardboard. Push a bone folder into the paper to emboss.

Travel

Use old maps to make envelopes or storage pockets.

Airmail envelope

Postage tags are a great way to incorporate handwritten notes.

Retrace your route with string and paper stars.

Use a combination of frames and photo corners to enhance your images.

Wedding

Edged
frame

Embossed
hearts

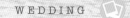

Gilding is a simple
embellishment
that's very effective.

Store confetti
as a keepsake.

Heart
box

Try making envelopes
from different materials.

Baby's first year

Paper bunting

Paper bow

Retro photo frame

Edged frame

Glue on buttons
as decorations.

Rosettes

Make miniature
papercuts and
put them in front
of coloured paper.

Templates

These templates can save you a bit of time when putting together your scrapbook. Scale them up or down to suit your needs.

Retro photo frames (pages 178–179)

Baby bunting (pages 180–181)

Fold along the dotted lines.

Heart envelope (pages 182–183)

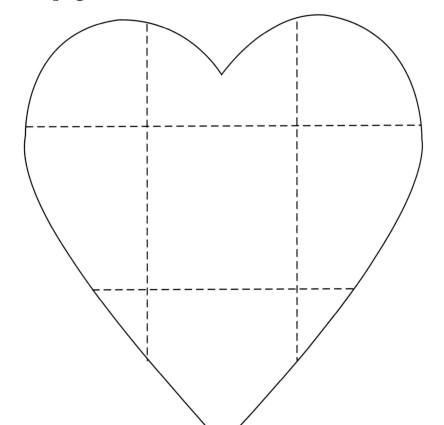

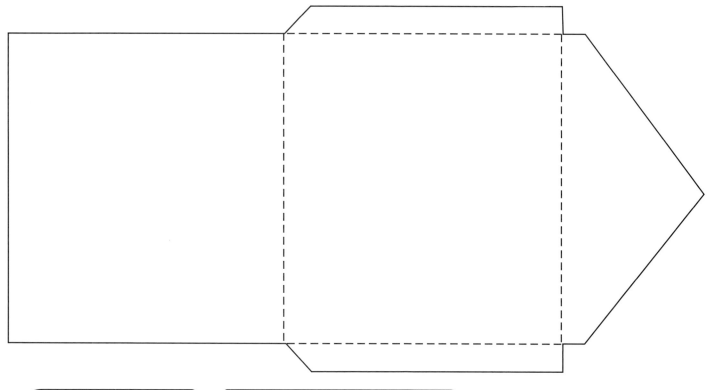

Envelope (page 191)

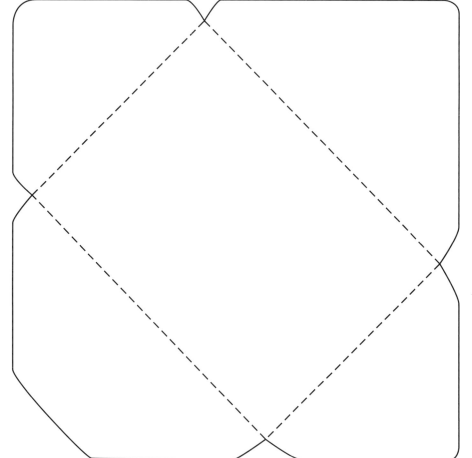

Bunting
(pages 180–181)

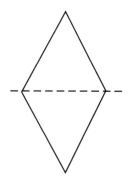

Envelope
(pages 182–183)

Templates

Pop-up bouquet (pages 14–19)

Enlarge to 145%

Score along
dotted lines

Leaf x 1

x 6

x 1

Edge x 2

Central flowers x 4

Pink central flower x 1

x 3

x 2

x 2

x 2

Feather gift tag (pages 20–23)

Enlarge to 125%

Score along
dotted lines

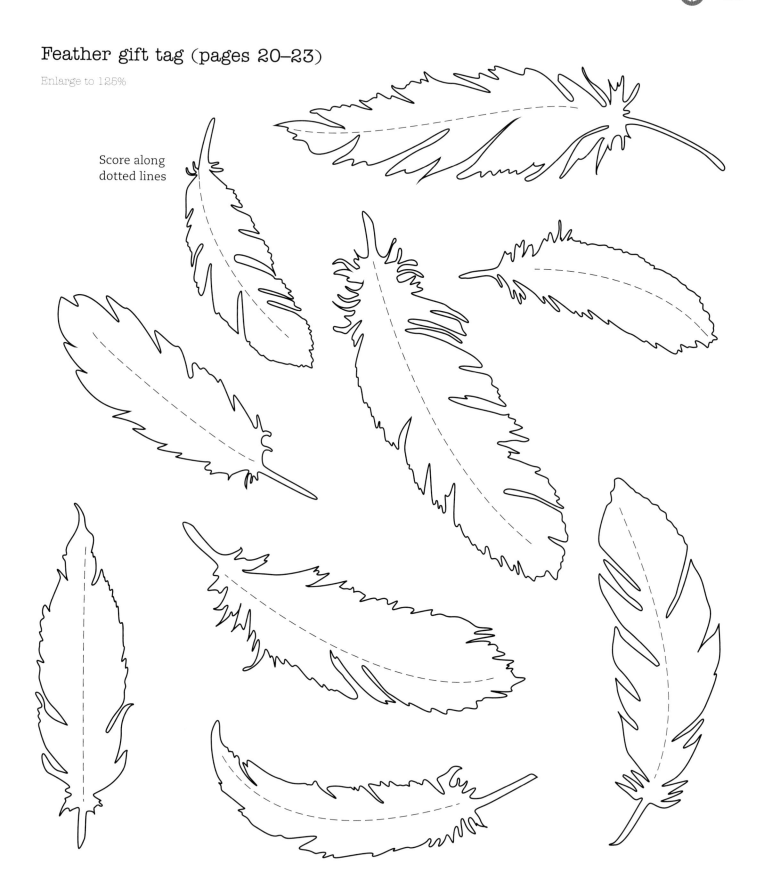

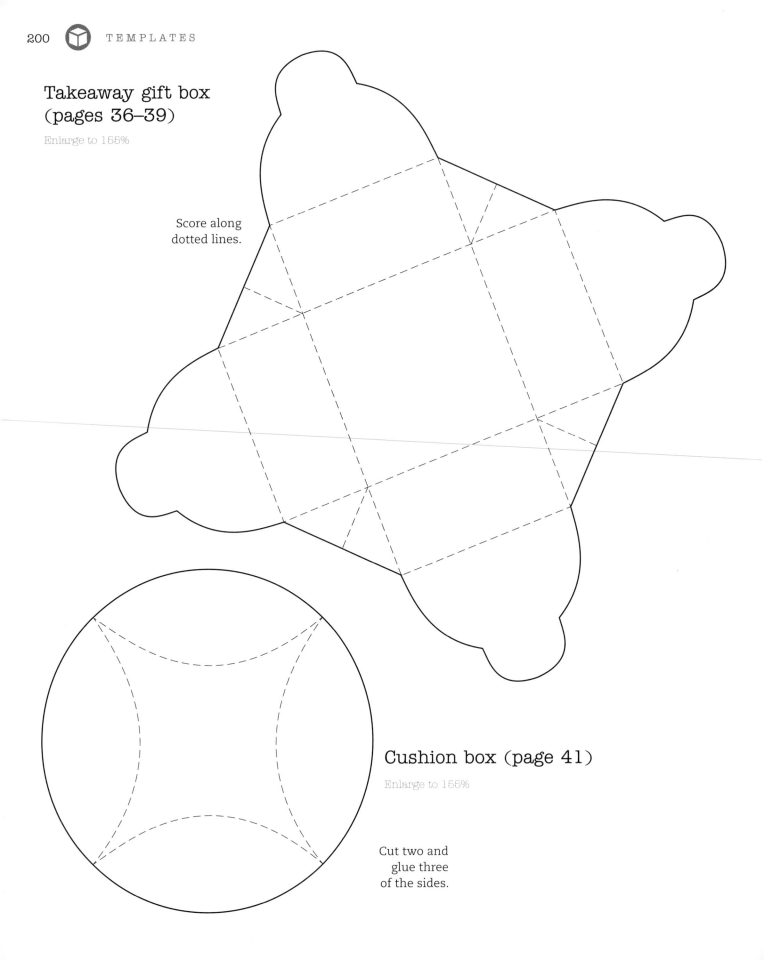

Takeaway gift box
(pages 36–39)

Enlarge to 155%

Score along
dotted lines.

Cushion box (page 41)

Enlarge to 155%

Cut two and
glue three
of the sides.

Pillow box (page 40)

Enlarge to 155%

3D star (pages 46–47)

Enlarge to 155%

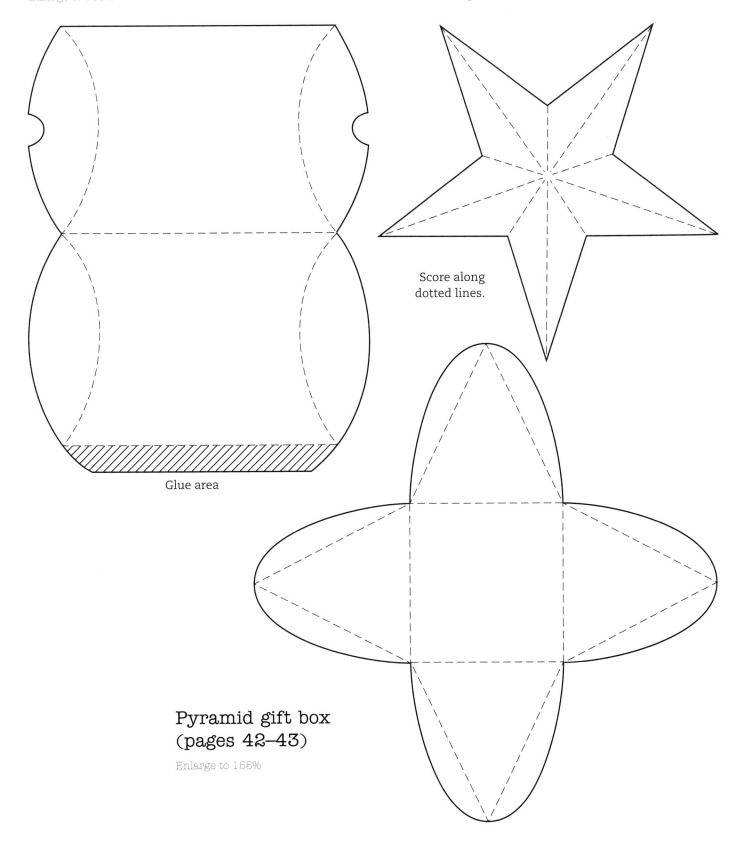

Score along
dotted lines.

Glue area

Pyramid gift box
(pages 42–43)

Enlarge to 155%

Layered papercut (pages 50–53)

Enlarge to 330%

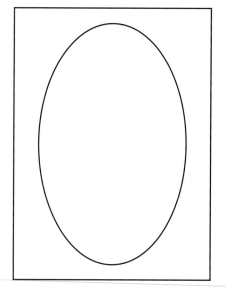

Grey border (optional)

Lilac

Yellow

Pink

White

Papercut variation (page 54)

Enlarge to 330%

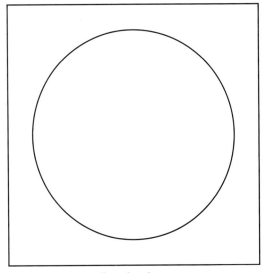

Grey border

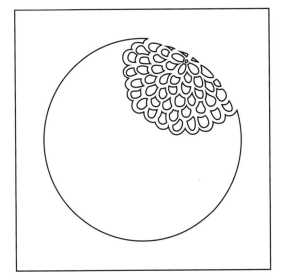

Pastel pink

Teal

Orange

White

Oval papercut variation (page 55)

Enlarge to 330%

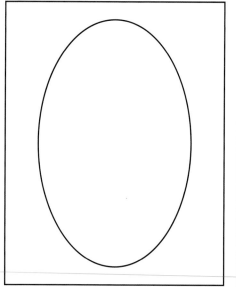

Grey border

Teal

Pastel pink

Orange

White

Nursery papercut (pages 60–63)

Actual size

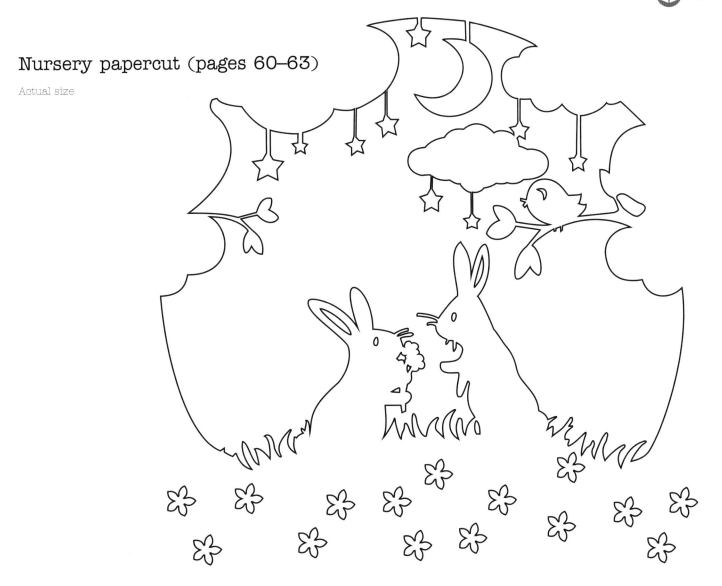

Snowflake bauble (pages 98–101)

Scale to fit the size of the bauble

Papercut locket (pages 64–65)

Scale to fit the size of the locket

Papercut lantern
(pages 66–69)

Enlarge to 120%

Koi carp lantern (pages 70–71)

Enlarge to 165%

Lily lantern (pages 70–71)

Enlarge to 200%

Bear mask (pages 108–111)

Actual size

Scale band to fit.

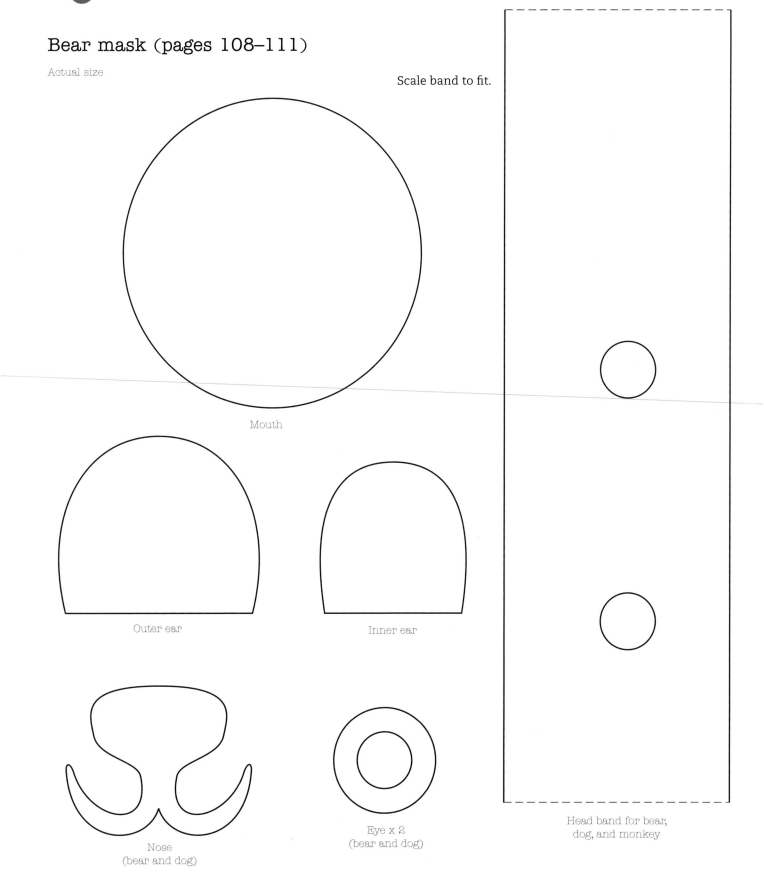

Mouth

Outer ear

Inner ear

Nose
(bear and dog)

Eye x 2
(bear and dog)

Head band for bear,
dog, and monkey

Dog mask (page 108)

Enlarge to 125%

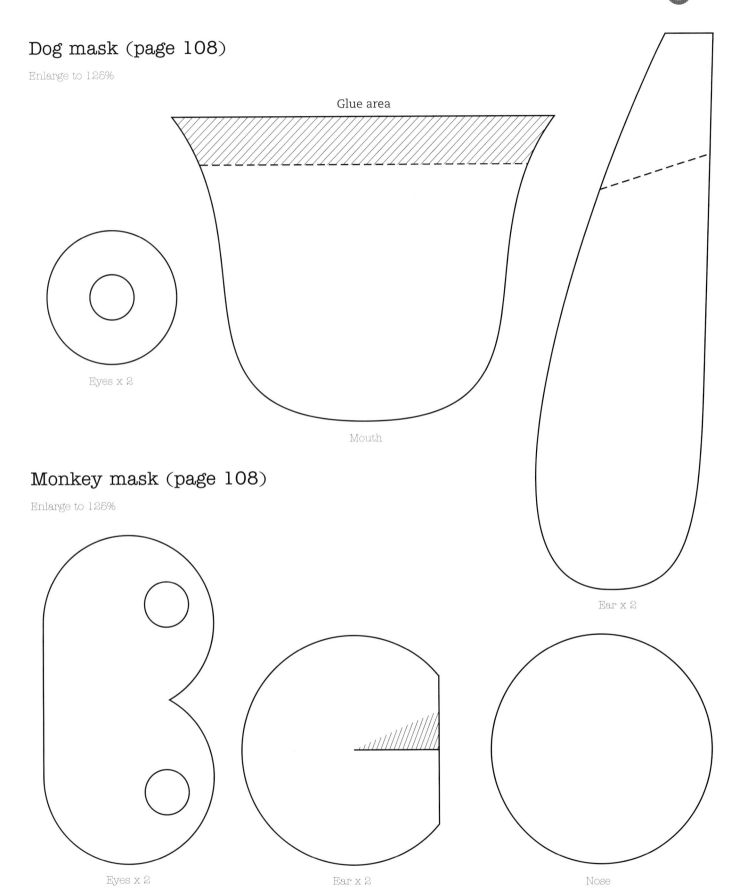

Glue area

Eyes x 2

Mouth

Monkey mask (page 108)

Enlarge to 125%

Ear x 2

Eyes x 2

Ear x 2

Nose

Nursery mobile (pages 112–117)

Actual size. Makes one owl.

Leaf x 4

Wing x 4

Score along
dotted lines.

Breast x 2

Eyes x 4

x 6

Body x 2

x 5

x 6

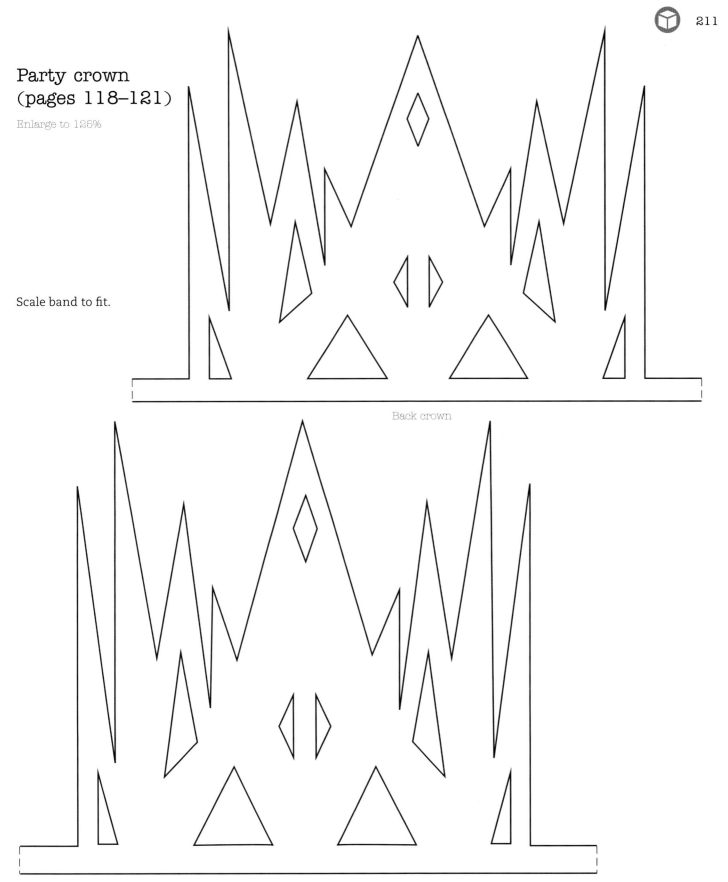

Party crown
(pages 118–121)

Enlarge to 125%

Scale band to fit.

Back crown

Front crown

Butterfly crown (page 118)

Enlarge to 125%

Scale band to fit.

Headdress (page 118)

Enlarge to 120%

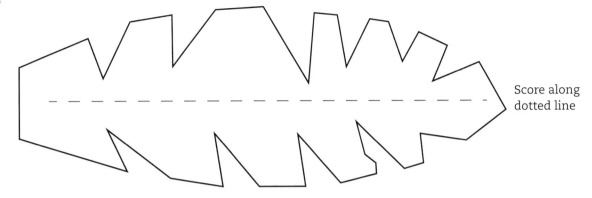

Score along
dotted line

Scale band to fit.

Star crown (page 118)

Enlarge to 120%

Scale band to fit.

Cherry blossom (pages 124–127)

Actual size

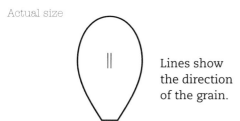

Lines show
the direction
of the grain.

Ranunculus (pages 132–135)

Actual size

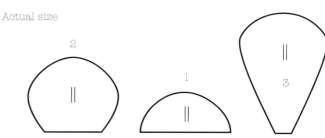

Peony (pages 128–131)

Actual size

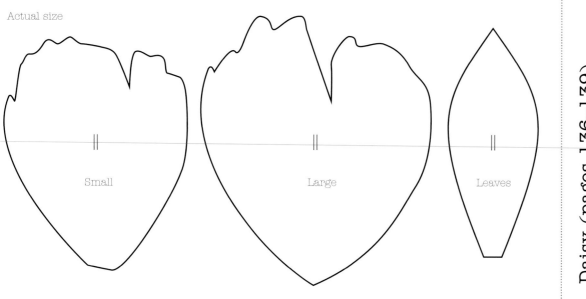

Small

Large

Leaves

Daisy (pages 136–139)

Actual size

Anemone (pages 140–143)

Actual size

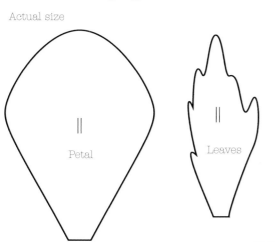

Petal

Leaves

Daffodil (pages 144–147)

Actual size

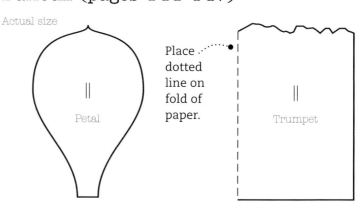

Petal

Place
dotted
line on
fold of
paper.

Trumpet

Daffodil leaves

Large rose (pages 148–151)

Enlarge to 155%

Small petal x 8

Large petal x 6

Sepals x 8

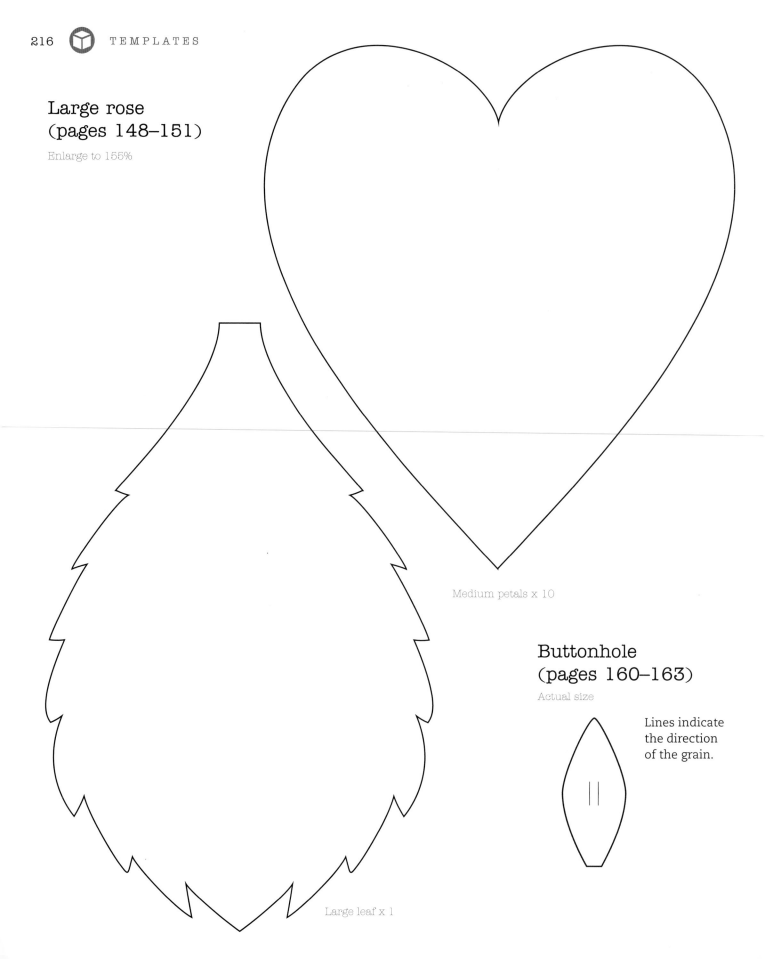

Large rose
(pages 148–151)

Enlarge to 155%

Medium petals x 10

Buttonhole
(pages 160–163)

Actual size

Lines indicate
the direction
of the grain.

Large leaf x 1

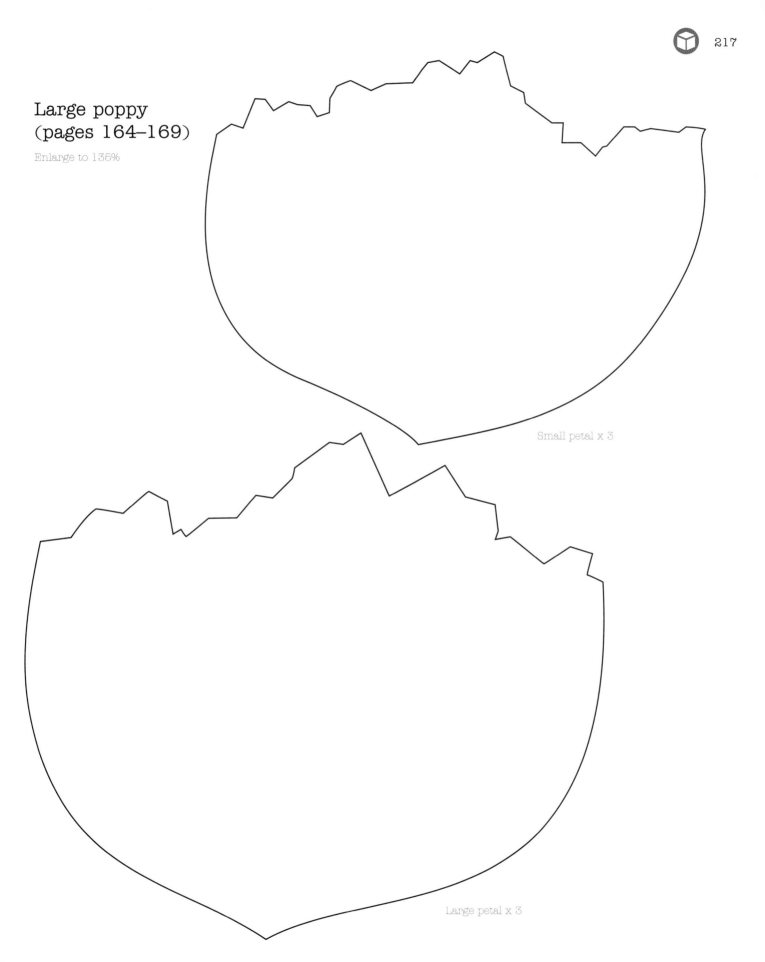

Large poppy
(pages 164–169)

Enlarge to 135%

Small petal x 3

Large petal x 3

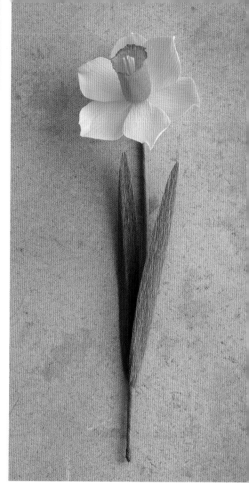

Index

Acknowledgments

The creative team would like to thank the following crafters for their hard work and expertise. We hope you are as inspired by their talent as we are.

Sophie Pelham

Pop-up bouquet

Nursery mobile

Motoko Sugawara

Origami fairy lights

Rochelle Falconer

Layered papercut

Square papercut

Oval papercut

Bryony Fripp

Feather gift tags

Takeaway gift boxes

Pillow boxes

Square boxes

Pyramid boxes

Sonia Moore

Customized paper

3D star tag

Origami birds

Bear mask

Monkey mask

Dog mask

Ria Holland

Quilled card

Gary Evans

Quilled earrings

Katie Aldous

Large rose

Holly Owst

Large poppy

Charlotte Bull

Photo corners and frames

Envelopes and pockets

Rosettes

Gilding and embossing

Travel scrapbook

Wedding scrapbook

Baby scrapbook

Danielle Gallagher

Papercut lanterns

Koi carp variation

Star crown

Floral crown

Spiky crown

Feather crown

Snowflake bauble

Martine Charalambou

Silhouette frames

Hanging garlands

Hanging fan

Susan Beech

Cherry blossom

Peony

Ranunculus

Daisy

Anemone

Daffodil

Wreath

Buttonholes

Festival headband

Emma Stevens

Nursery papercut

Papercut locket

Clare Shedden

Honeycomb pom-pom

DK would also like to thank

Marie Lorimer for preparing the index. Claire Cordier and Lucy Claxton for picture library assistance. Andy Crawford for photographing the pom-pom project. Paperchase for the loan of props for the fans project. Olive and Florence Pugsley, Aeden Jenkins, Carlow and Devon Day-Lewis, Tyler-Justin, Alighla and Isabella Gallagher for modelling. Tilly Lee, Danielle Glover, and Alice Bowsher for hand-modelling.